TALES FROM THE
BALTIMORE ORIOLES
DUGOUT

A COLLECTION OF THE GREATEST ORIOLES STORIES EVER TOLD

LOUIS BERNEY

SPORTS
PUBLISHING

Sports Publishing books may be purchased in bulk at special discounts for sales promotion, corporate gifts, fund-raising, or educational purposes. Special editions can also be created to specifications. For details, contact the Special Sales Department, Sports Publishing, 307 West 36th Street, 11th Floor, New York, NY 10018 or sportspubbooks@skyhorsepublishing.com.

Sports Publishing® is a registered trademark of Skyhorse Publishing, Inc.®, a Delaware corporation.

Visit our website at www.sportspubbooks.com

10 9 8 7 6 5 4 3 2 1

Library of Congress Cataloging-in-Publication Data is available on file.

ISBN: 978-1-61321-087-1

Printed in the United States of America

To my mother, Carla Berney, who became an Orioles fan after coming to the United States from Europe, and to my daughter, Melissa Berney, who was born an Orioles fan.

Acknowledgments

I would like to thank Bob Brown for the immense help he offered me in the preparation of this book. Bob was a longtime director of public relations for the Orioles and probably has a greater sense of the team's history than any person on earth. He unflinchingly shared his invaluable files with me, and for this, as well as his friendship and selfless contributions to Baltimore Orioles baseball, I am very grateful.

Contents

Introduction

When the modern-day Orioles were in their infancy, I was a kid growing up in northwest Baltimore. Baseball and I shared a certain innocence back then. Players didn't make millions of dollars. In fact, a number of Orioles—including stars like Jim Palmer, Boog Powell and Dave McNally—had to take jobs during the off-season to pay their rent. Palmer and McNally and several others worked as salesmen at my father's clothing store.

Most of the players of that era rented apartments near Memorial Stadium. None lived in overgrown estates out in the horse country or in high-rises on Baltimore's downtown waterfront. Orioles then often resided in Baltimore year-round. The city was their home. They were full-time members of the Baltimore community, and the community considered them as their adopted sons, as members of the Baltimore family.

In the earliest years, during the 1950s, the Orioles weren't very good. But it didn't matter. We were just happy to have a team in Baltimore. The team might lose game after game, but hope soared every time the club signed a new bonus baby or eked out a win over the mighty Yankees. When four different Orioles pitchers hurled consecutive shutouts in 1957, we were on top of the world. When Hoyt Wilhelm no-hit the Yankees on a wet afternoon at Memorial Stadium, those few of us in the ballpark that day experienced baseball nirvana. And when Billy O'Dell was the most valuable player in the first major-league All-Star game ever played in Baltimore in 1958, the city could barely contain its pride.

Since the Orioles never were a winner during the 1950s, the losses never really seemed that bitter. And the victories they were able to cobble together—especially those, once again, over the hated and feared Yankees—were oh so sweet.

It might be hard to imagine in today's world of sports-as-big-business, but the Orioles and their players back then really were like members of the family—my family and thousands of others throughout the city. Elderly grandmothers knew the names of second-string infielders on the team and doted over their images.

The Orioles were an integral part of my life as I was going through my childhood. I fell asleep listening to night games on a transistor radio that I hid from my parents under my blanket. And if I didn't know whether the team had won or lost when I woke up in the morning—there was no ESPN or 11 o'clock sports in that era—I'd run outside in my pajamas to get the morning newspaper and tantalize myself, cautiously and painstakingly looking at the box score, inning-by-inning, to find out whether they'd pulled a victory out of their caps.

My brother, David, and I would ride two different Baltimore buses—transferring at Falls Road and 41st Street—to the stadium on 33rd Street to attend games. Parents had no fear back then of allowing their young children to travel throughout the city by themselves. If we didn't have tickets in advance, we could buy them for 75 cents. There was never a problem getting seats in the 1950s and even the 1960s and '70s. Games were never sold out. And David and I would relish the excitement of daring to sneak down into the best seats, which also were largely vacant.

I saw scores of thrilling games in my youth, and probably even more insignificant and routine ones, details of which I can still remember as though they were played just yesterday. Every time I went to the stadium and saw its huge brick facade looming in front of me, a thrill raced through my body. Memorial Stadium was the temple of my youth.

In those days, there was no anger or venom directed at the ball club. Expectations were nonexistent, but the possibilities for success and greatness that we concocted in our minds were vast. I'd listen to games or watch them on television in the library of our house, swinging a bat as I hung onto every pitch, fantasizing that I was the one standing in the batter's box for the Orioles. When Heywood Sullivan of the Red Sox hit a ninth-inning home run one day to snatch victory from the hometown boys, I angrily took a swipe at the chandelier in the library, knocking out a light or two or three.

I wanted nothing more in life than for the Orioles to win.

Even though as kids we felt a close bond with the players, we really didn't know much about them personally. We never would have suspected that they had personal peccadilloes or character flaws. Yet we still felt as though we knew them intimately. I never thought of the players as anything but demigods. I could cite every batting average and every ERA. We didn't know—or even consider—how much they got paid or what type of contracts they had. All we cared about was what they did on the field, or, if we might get lucky, gaining an autograph when the players left the ballpark after games. It wasn't really the autograph that meant much. It was the opportunity to have personal contact with the players, even if it was nothing more than sticking out a hand with the scrap of paper for them to sign.

The Orioles seemed to have fun back then. Life was not as serious, as burdensome as it is today. The players lived and died baseball. They didn't have stock portfolios, agents or reputations to worry about. Baseball was a game for the players, not a business.

And that's what this book is largely about.

When I interviewed players for the book, many of whom were my childhood idols, they looked back on their time in an Orioles uniform as a wonderful epoch in their life.

Oh, they tried to win and they did have to worry about staying in the big leagues. But they went about their playing careers with an insouciance that is sadly absent from today's game. They were, as Roy Campanella of the Dodgers sagely observed, men with a lot of little boy in them. They did not take themselves too seriously.

This is a trait I admire in one of the greatest Orioles of recent years, Cal Ripken Jr. Ripken grew up in the Orioles family of the past, when his father was a manager in the club's minor league system. He embodied many of the characteristics of the old Orioles. In public, especially in his last few seasons with the team, Ripken came across as a serious and well-rehearsed speaker. But in the Orioles clubhouse, and even on the field, he loved the game and played it like a boy. He was one of the team's great pranksters and fun-lovers. Unlike many of today's ballplayers, Ripken has always been a true fan of the sport himself. To Ripken, baseball has been not only a game but also a passion.

In compiling the book I was impressed with how sharp the players' memories were. These men who appeared in hundreds or thousands of games could recall a specific at-bat or inning—pitch by pitch—that I might ask about from 20, 30 or 40 years ago.

Even when the Orioles became good—and for 30 years they had the best won-lost record in baseball—they had fun as a team. The Orioles truly were a family. They played together both on and off the field. And what they miss the most from those days, they told me, is the camaraderie of their teammates.

I didn't really have to do much writing for this book. Most of the words that appear are from the players themselves. In sharing their stories, they rekindled the joy and excitement of baseball that was so much a part of my youth. I am indebted to the players for sharing with me their exploits on the field—both in person, when I was watching them as a boy, and in the tales they told me for this book.

CHAPTER 1

"Bullet Bob" Heads North: Bob Turley
(1954)

B
ob Turley was the first real star to play for the modern-day Orioles. A big right-hander who could throw a ball through the proverbial barn door, he was the Orioles' lone All-Star representative in their first season back in Baltimore in 1954. Although the team was a wobbly 54-100 that first season at Memorial Stadium, Turley went 14-15 with a 3.46 ERA and led the American League in strikeouts with 185.

After the season, the club's new manager/general manager, Paul Richards, traded Turley to the Yankees in a 17-player deal. Turley became a dominant pitcher in New York, but the trade, which brought players like Gus Triandos, Gene Woodling and Willie Miranda to Baltimore, began the gradual formation of the Orioles into a competitive team based on Richards' formula of strong pitching and airtight defense.

Turley spent just that first debut season in Baltimore, but he remembers it as a welcome relief from the dismal final days when he played for the St. Louis Browns before they became the Orioles.

"When we came over from St. Louis, it was an exciting time for us because we weren't drawing any [fans] in St. Louis. And the fans came out for us in Baltimore. We drew a million people that year. The fans were excited, and so were we.

"I pitched the first home game in Baltimore. Clint Courtney hit the first home run, and then Vern Stephens hit a two-run homer to win it for us, 3-1. When you pitch nine innings in a game like that and get the win, it was a thrill. I was just a young guy then.

"I remember in the clubhouse thinking even though we put on a new uniform, we were still the St. Louis Browns. There wasn't that much of a change in our team. We didn't win a lot of games that year, but we did lose quite a few.

"I remember one game when Billy Hunter was playing shortstop and the other team had a man on second. Dick Kryhoski was our first baseman. Billy made one hell of a play on a ground ball hit up the middle to catch the ball. He turned around and threw a strike to first base. The only problem was, nobody was there. Kryhoski had thought it was going to be a base hit, so he went to the mound to make the cutoff play.

"There were a lot of old ball players on that team. Vern Stephens was a real idol of mine, because I had grown up in St. Louis. Vic Wertz was there for a little while. And then there was Clint Courtney. Clint was a real character. They called him 'Old Scrap Iron.' He'd run hard and slide hard into bases and get your team in fights.

"When we first came to Baltimore, the fans were giving a lot of prizes and gifts to the ball players. I'd just come out of the military in '53, so it was all very exciting to me. Well, we had a meeting in the clubhouse to decide what to do with all those prizes, whether we would divide them up or let them go to whom they were supposed to. Clint got up in the front of the room in the clubhouse to talk about the different gifts. 'If you think I'm going to give you donkeys anything, you're crazy,' he said. And that's how the meeting ended.

"Clint wore pitchers out by throwing the ball so hard back to us. Some guys let the balls go right by into the outfield, so they didn't have to catch them.

Bob Turley. *Baltimore Orioles Photos*

"I also pitched the first night game for the Orioles at Memorial Stadium a few days later. There were more than 43,000 people at the park. I had a no-run, no-hit game against the Indians going into the ninth inning. I got one out, and then Al Rosen hit a single between short and third. Larry Doby then hit a high fly ball down the right-field line, and it just got into the stands. They had that short wall right down the line [309 feet], and the ball he hit just barely got into the stands. So I lost the game, 2-1.

"I wasn't that upset about losing the no-hitter. You'd like to have it, but no-hitters are just one game. Another pitcher from another team had a no-hitter around then and got sent to the minors two months later. How you pitch over a long period of time is the important thing.

"Coming off the field after the first game that we won, it was different then. We didn't jump up and down. I just remember Vern Stephens and Clint Courtney coming over to congratulate me. I went into the clubhouse then and talked to Bobo Newsom [a former big league pitcher and early Baltimore broadcaster]. He interviewed me after that first game. It was good getting off to a good start.

"Before we came home, we had split the first two games of the season in Detroit. Duane Pillette won, and Don Larsen lost, so after I won, we were 2-1—right on top. We came into Baltimore from Detroit by train, and it was raining. We got right off the train, and then we got into convertibles and rode to the ballpark. It rained right up to the game time. I remember the big crowds of people on the streets greeting us. It was really exciting.

"I pitched a lot of baseball that year, and right near the end of the season, Paul Richards, who had just been named as general manager, asked me not to pitch at the end of the season. He said, 'You have nothing to gain, but you could hurt your arm.' Jimmy Dykes was still the manager then, and he came to me and said, 'We could have you pitch, Bob, but it's probably better for you if you don't.' I was 14-15 and was trying to even my record to 15-15. Inside my heart, I wanted to pitch, but when you're a ball player, and you have your manager and your general manager telling you not to pitch, you pay attention. So I didn't pitch, and I ended up 14-15.

"After the season I took a job working for the Hecht Company in Towson. I was staying in Baltimore for the winter. Richards talked to me and said I was going to be one of the players they'd build the club around the next year. But then within 30 days, they traded me to the Yankees with Billy Hunter and Don Larsen.

"I remember real well how I heard about the trade. My son was born October 25 that year, and I was sitting watching television and feeding my son. Suddenly it flashed on the screen and said, 'Bob Turley, multiple players traded to the New York Yankees.' That's how I found out I was traded. No one from the club called me to tell me. I don't think they ever called me."

CHAPTER 2

The Early Days:
Joe Durham
(1954; 1957)

When Joe Durham arrived in Baltimore in September of 1954, he became the first African American to play in the field for the Orioles. Baseball was vastly different then from the way it is today, and so were the Orioles—a ragtag team composed mostly of journeymen who were on the downside of their careers. The club had a few good pitchers but hitting was mediocre at best. The 1954 club had a team batting average of .251 and hit a total of just 52 home runs—only two more than Brady Anderson alone hit for the Orioles in 1996. Lacking both youth and speed, they stole a mere 30 bases—again, less than Luis Aparicio, Anderson and a handful of other Orioles have since swiped in a single season.

"We had a mixture of players. We had players other teams probably couldn't use. It was a very, very weak team. I think the biggest asset, though, was pitching. There was good pitching with [Bob] Turley, [Don] Larsen, Joe Coleman—guys like that. Hitting-wise, with that big ballpark in Baltimore, the ball didn't carry well. Forty-six RBIs led the club, eight home runs led the club, so there wasn't much offense at all.

5

"There were some funny guys though. Ray Murray, a catcher—'The Deacon,' they used to call him—was a very, very funny guy. And Clint Courtney was there also. He was just a funny character. You could just look at Courtney and start to laugh. He came back to the Orioles a few years later, and he bought a brand new car from a used car dealer, Johnny Wilbanks, in Baltimore. In those days you usually didn't have air conditioning in the cars. It was a brand new Cadillac that he bought, and it was a very warm July day. And he comes into the clubhouse. He never, never perspired, but this day he's perspiring and he's raging about the man selling him a car that didn't have air conditioning. He said the knobs were broken on the door, so he couldn't roll the windows down. So Skinny Brown went out to the parking lot to check it out. And he came back, and he fell into the middle of the floor laughing. He said the car had automatic windows, and Courtney just didn't know how to operate them. He was a funny man.

"I came up to the team late that year—Ryne Duren, Frank Kellert and I. We came from San Antonio in September. All three of us had good years there. And the players had such a poor year in Baltimore, the old veterans kind of were just looking at us. In my third game I hit my first home run. But the team just wasn't going anywhere. The team lost 100 games that year. It was one of the poorest Baltimore teams.

"The manager was Jimmy Dykes. He was a character. He'd sit there with his legs crossed and a big cigar hanging out of his mouth. He didn't bother you. He was at the end of his managerial career. I think he just wanted to go home and sit on a rocking chair. He was very cool, very calm. He didn't have too much to say.

"Jehosie Heard, a pitcher, was the first black to play for the Orioles. I was the first black position player. We had another black at San Antonio, Harry Wilson, but he was a pitcher. I was the only one out on the field every night. So I was the one who took all the abuse from the fans down there. It was mainly name-calling, which didn't bother me. As long as you don't put your hands on me, I'm fine. In Shreveport, in particular, they were very, very rough on me. I played left field, and right by left field there were the bleacher seats for whites only. They constantly called me all kinds

Joe Durham. *Brace Photo*

of names and talked about my parents. I'm from Newport News, Virginia, and here I am in Shreveport, Louisiana—now, what in the world did these people know about my parents? Nothing. So you just take these things. You don't pay attention.

"Actually, they came out to see me. Because every time we were going to Shreveport, those bleachers were loaded. And I had some of my best games there. Nothing like that happened in the major leagues. The only thing in the major leagues was that in a lot of places, you couldn't stay with your teammates. That makes it kind of tough. People don't realize that baseball is a family game. On your off days, families would get together and have picnics and cookouts and whatnot. But being on a team where you have to stay across town, and you don't see your teammates until you go to the ballpark, it takes something out of you. You have to work extra hard, or that much harder, to try to be successful. In 1954, blacks couldn't stay at hotels with their teammates in cities like Washington, Chicago and Baltimore. Detroit, Boston, New York and Philadelphia were okay. In Chicago, the Orioles stayed at the Edgewater Hotel. I had to stay at the Evans Hotel at 161st and Evans. I'll never forget that.

"Jehosie was gone when I got to Baltimore, so I was the only black on the team when I got to Baltimore. I had already gotten used to being by myself a lot in strange towns—in Texas and throughout Oklahoma. You're by yourself, so you learn how to do things by yourself. I used to write a lot of letters. There were no televisions in the rooms those days. Telephones were unheard of. I stayed in a lot of places they called 'tourist homes.' It was nothing but a two-story house with one bathroom and bathtub downstairs somewhere. I couldn't stay with my teammates at the hotels downtown. I couldn't ride in the same cab. When I first came to Baltimore, Don Larsen was my means of getting to and from the ballpark. He had a brand new, 1954 Oldsmobile, and he used to pick me up down on Pennsylvania Avenue in front of the casino. And he'd drop me off there at night when he came back. I would have had to catch a cab, because I couldn't afford to have an automobile in those days.

"Larsen was a real loosey-goosey type person. He liked to have a lot of fun. He liked to drink and enjoy himself. Turley was a little on the quiet side, a very serious-minded person. They were two pretty good pitchers. Turley had an excellent arm. Now some guys throw 95-96. I don't know exactly what he threw back then, but he had to be in that group. He just had an explosive fastball. Larsen had very good control and threw hard, but that was the year he won three and lost 21. But nothing seemed to bother Don Larsen. I think he was happy when he was traded to New York, where he got some run support. He didn't have any run support in Baltimore."

CHAPTER 3

The First Bonus Baby: Billy O'Dell
(1954-1959)

B illy O'Dell was the first young player the Orioles ever signed. He was a left-handed pitcher who had finished his junior year at Clemson University in 1954, and he went to Baltimore and signed on June 8 of the same year. He returned to South Carolina to pick up his belongings and rejoined the ball club in Boston. O'Dell not only was the Orioles' first young acquisition, but he also became their first bonus baby. Bonus babies were young players who signed for at least $4,000 and, at the time, had to remain on the major league roster for two years. O'Dell never pitched a day in the minor leagues.

But he also didn't get much action with the Orioles at the beginning.

"Back then they thought to pitch in the big leagues you needed at least five years' experience in the minor leagues. I didn't have any minor-league experiences. So I sat on the bench from June until almost August of 1954 before I even got into a game. I came in as a reliever. Then I got my first start in September. In my second start, on the next to the last day of the season, I was pitching against Virgil Trucks of the White Sox. Virgil was going

10

Billy O'Dell. *Baltimore Orioles Photos*

for his 20th win, and I was going for my first. In fact, he was supposed to pitch the next day, but when the Orioles announced I was going to pitch, they moved him up a day, probably because they thought it would be easier for him to get his win against a rookie. I beat him, 2-1. I pitched nine innings. That was my first win in the big leagues."

The left-handed O'Dell was drafted into the military and missed almost two full years of baseball. But shortly after he returned, he pitched well enough to be selected to be part of the 1958 American League All-Star team. The honor was especially meaningful because the game was played in Baltimore that summer, and O'Dell and catcher Gus Triandos were the two local representatives on the squad. Triandos was the starting catcher, and when American League All-Star manager Casey Stengel of the Yankees removed him from the game, the crowd booed lustily. Stengel, however, would get his chance to win back the crowd's affections after the sixth inning.

"When I was chosen for the All-Star team, I didn't expect to get in the game. But I always pitched pretty good against the Yankees, and Casey always liked me. We got a call down in the bullpen for someone to warm up, so Billy Pierce of the White Sox got up and started throwing. But then Casey called back and said, 'No, I want O'Dell to get up.' That call surprised me. And being in Baltimore, the fans just went wild when I started warming up. I pitched the seventh, eighth and ninth innings and didn't allow a man on base. That was back when they tried to win the All-Star game. It was really exciting. I'd been in baseball just a few years, since I'd missed time in the military.

"After the game, I was selected as the most valuable player, and that made the whole thing even more exciting. That was the first MVP award ever given in the All-Star game. It was the 25th anniversary of the game. They brought a trophy to my locker and just gave it to me. It wasn't such a big deal then. Now I think they get a car. Things have changed."

O'Dell also hit one of the most memorable—and unusual—home runs in the history of Memorial Stadium. It came on May 19, 1959, his last season with the Orioles (he was traded to the

Giants the next year). The ball he hit traveled no more than 120 feet in the air. O'Dell and the White Sox's Pierce were engaged in a tight pitchers' duel when O'Dell, known as "Digger," came to the plate near the end of the game. The score was tied, 1-1.

"Billy threw me a curve ball, and I hit it on the end of the bat. It just went right over the first baseman's head. The right fielder [Al Smith] was coming in on the ball, and it hit the foul line, which was then made of wood. So the ball bounced off the wood and kept on going down the line. There was a rubber hose out by the right field wall, and when the ball got to the wall, instead of bouncing right back, it followed along the hose, rolling straight down the path of the hose. Everyone was coming in and the ball was going out. It was just a fluke thing. I was in too big a hurry running around the bases to know exactly what had happened. But it turned out to be a home run, and we won, 2-1."

CHAPTER 4

The O's First Slugger:
Gus Triandos
(1955-1962)

During their early years in the mid-1950s, the Orioles had a dearth of power hitters. The team's top home run hitter in the club's very first season in the American League was veteran third baseman Vern Stephens. He hit a grand total of eight homers during that year. The entire club had but 52 home runs in 1954. But before the 1955 season, the Orioles obtained catcher Gus Triandos from the Yankees. He was their only legitimate slugger during that early era of Baltimore baseball. Over each of the next five years Triandos led the club in homers, and in four of those years he also was the Orioles' top RBI man. He tied an American League record in 1958 for home runs by a catcher, with 30 round-trippers.

"Tying the record for home runs by a catcher meant a lot. I didn't think it would last as long as it did. I didn't realize it was a record for catchers in the American League, until it was written about."

Playing in Baltimore for eight seasons was not always easy or enjoyable for Triandos. Fans seemed to expect him to bash a home run every time he stepped to the plate. When the lumbering

14

Gus Triandos. *Baltimore Orioles Photos*

catcher instead either struck out or hit into a double play, he heard plenty of boos from the hometown crowd. Triandos also was stymied by the huge dimensions of Memorial Stadium, especially the deep fences in the power alleys and in centerfield.

"Fans got on me every chance they had. Living in Baltimore, I met some of the best people I've ever met in my life, but there's always the bad with the good, and there's always some people that don't like you. I would have liked to have left Baltimore earlier than I did. It was a big ballpark and a tough place to play. They seemed to boo big guys in Baltimore.

"Things were up and down for me. You had some good days and some bad days. Now, I think playing baseball was the greatest thing I did. I'm glad I did play ball. But then, there were bad things. And when you were going bad, it felt terrible. And sometimes the downs made you not feel so good.

"Most of the people there were nice, especially the ones who bought the season tickets. It was most of the free ticket guys who were the worst.

"Memorial Stadium made you a worse hitter, because you tried to pull the ball too much. The fences were 422 feet to left center. It went out to 420 real fast, and that was tough, too."

Not only were the outfield fences a good distance from home, but so was the screen behind the plate. Triandos was not a fast runner, and he spent considerable time chasing balls to the backstop. That was because he had the unenviable task of catching Hoyt Wilhelm, whose famous knuckleball was at least as tough to catch as it was to hit. During the years in the late 1950s and early 1960s when Wilhelm pitched for the Orioles, Triandos routinely led the American League in passed balls. In 1959, he was charged with 28 passed balls. Virtually all came while Wilhelm was on the mound.

Manager Paul Richards, who never had a shortage of novel ideas for helping make the Orioles a stronger team, devised a special catcher's mitt to be used while Wilhelm pitched. It was almost twice the normal size. Triandos used it until baseball officials finally outlawed Richards' oversized glove.

"It used to be a hell of a long run back to the backstop to pick up a passed ball. It was hot in Baltimore, we had heavy uniforms, and a lot of times because of the long run back to the backstop, it got to be very physically tiring to play there.

"You had two or three passed balls a game when Hoyt pitched, and you caught 90 others. But it was the passed balls that got to be written about. Even when I warmed him up if I missed balls that he threw, I got booed.

"The big glove helped a lot. But it was hard to get the ball out of the glove when you tried to throw out a runner. Your hand would hit the glove while you tried to throw. It made it easier to catch, but harder to throw. They only used the glove for one or two years, and then they ruled that it had to be cut down to half its size.

"Richards was a strange guy. You never got too intimate with him. A lot of times he'd tell [coach] Luman Harris what to do instead of talking directly to the players. I never had long conversations with the guy. I never had any problems with him. He was strange, though. He wasn't a palsy-walsy guy, I guess."

Wilhelm, a member of baseball's Hall of Fame, might have been something of a challenge for Triandos, but he was an outstanding pitcher for the Orioles. Richards had the foresight to use Wilhelm as a starter rather than as a reliever, as almost all his other managers had done. In 1959, the year in which Wilhelm had more than half of his career starts, he went 15-11 for the Orioles and led the league with a 2.19 ERA.

He also pitched Baltimore's first no-hitter on September 20, 1958, against the Yankees. Triandos was behind the plate that afternoon and hit a home run—his record-tying 30th—to help Wilhelm beat New York, 1-0. There were fewer than 11,000 fans in the stadium that day.

"You don't realize until late in the game that it's a no-hitter. It really was not at all different from catching Wilhelm in any other game. It's always tough. You have to worry about balls getting by you. I didn't know until the late innings what was happening. The home run I hit was to dead center. I didn't think it was going to be the game winner. I think it was off Bobby Shantz.

"It was a damp day, and it had been raining. The no-hitter meant more to Hoyt than it did to me. He was a little older than anyone else. I didn't hang around with him, but I got along with him okay.

"After it gets to a certain inning, and a guy has a no-hitter, nobody says anything. You stay away from him, and you keep quiet. Nothing was said about it in the dugout. You don't want to jinx him. It was a 1-0 game, so the tension was there, but I didn't think the tension was because of the no-hitter, but because of the closeness of the game."

CHAPTER 5

The Human Highlight Reel:
Brooks Robinson
(1955-1977)

For 20 years, Brooks Robinson was the Baltimore Orioles. He was the first great player the team developed through its farm system. A teenager from Little Rock, Arkansas, he was a fan favorite almost as soon as he joined the team, not only because of his extraordinary glove and potent bat, but also because of his joyful demeanor and his delight at playing baseball. But for most of his early career, he was a secret gem enjoyed almost exclusively by Baltimore fans. It wasn't until the Orioles moved to the national stage by playing in the World Series that Robinson was fully appreciated by baseball fans across the country.

Robinson's miraculous performance in the 1970 World Series against Cincinnati transformed him into a superstar. He hit .429 and bashed two home runs with five RBIs in the five-game Series, but it was his glove work that elevated him to the level of baseball legend. Every ball hit within a country mile of third was gobbled up by Robinson; then whether from his knees or from the ground, he impossibly threw out every Reds batter who had the misfortune of hitting a ball his way.

"That was a very unusual World Series, because as an infielder you can play a week or two weeks and never get a chance to do anything spectacular or outstanding. And that particular World Series, I played almost 23 years professionally, and I don't think I ever had five games in a row like that, with the chance to make so many good plays. And I was hitting well, too. So it was a once-in-a-lifetime five-game series, and it just happened to be the World Series. That's the way I look at it. It was very unusual.

"That's the first time we'd ever played on Astroturf, and I think the big question when we went out to Cincinnati was, 'What kind of shoes are you going to wear—turf shoes, regular shoes?' And I ended up wearing regular spikes. Playing on Astroturf, you can take 10 or 15 minutes of ground balls, and you're going to be as good as you're going to get. There wasn't a whole lot of difference. I always felt if you played on Astroturf, you're going to be a better fielder and you'd be a better hitter. You're going to get more hits, just because the ball gets through the infield more. It's quicker. And defensively, there's no bad hops. You can go after balls a little differently than you would if you're on natural turf. So it was just one of those things that happened to be in the World Series. I think people who are not even baseball fans watch the World Series to see what's going on. So it was a big moment for me."

Robinson also was a mainstay of the first Orioles team to play in a World Series in 1966. He and Frank Robinson were the stars of that young team, which upset the more established Dodgers in a four-game sweep. What was truly remarkable about that 1966 World Series was that the Orioles scored more runs in the first inning of the very first game than the Dodgers were able to score in the entire Series. With one out in the top of the first during the first game at Chavez Ravine, Frank Robinson hit a two-run homer. Brooks Robinson was the very next batter, and he followed with a home run, giving the Orioles a 3-0 lead before there were even two outs in the Series. The Dodgers scored two runs that game but were shut out by young Orioles pitchers Jim Palmer, Wally Bunker and Dave McNally in the final three games.

Robinson remembers how exhilarating it was for the team to clinch the American League pennant in 1966 and win Baltimore's first berth in a World Series.

Brooks Robinson. *Baltimore Orioles Photos*

"We'd been waiting a long time for that. I guess I'd been waiting longer than anyone else, because I came to the Orioles in '55, right out of high school. I was up and down for three or four years. We had a shot to do it in '60 and didn't quite make it. In '64 we got even closer, and '66, that culminated in the win, going into the World Series with a couple weeks to spare. We had a celebration. It really was wonderful. [Trainer] Ralph Salvon was there, [trainer] Eddie Weidner was there, and we just had a good time. I knew that I wasn't going to play the next day. I was going to take the next day off. So we had a great trip to California and did a little celebrating. We'd waited a long time for that.

"When you're a youngster and sign a professional contract—I did when I was 18—you dream about playing in the minor leagues, making it to the major leagues, winning the pennant and winning the World Series. And if you get into the World Series, and you win, I think you say, 'If it never happens again, this is what it was all about.' You've done it once and realized your dream. That's what it really meant to me. I get a big smile on my face when I think about each one of those guys on that special team, and on every World Series. I always say, if you're around long enough, someone's going to get you or you're going to get them. I played in four World Series. The two we were supposed to win, we lost, and the two we were supposed to lose, we won. That's what it's all about, playing in the World Series. If you win, that makes it even nicer. That's what it's all about."

Robinson played in his early years for manager Paul Richards, a man who had a brilliant baseball mind and exhibited a dramatic aloofness toward his players. Players under Richards all admired and respected him for his understanding of the game. But none of them ever felt any closeness toward him. He always kept a distance between himself and his players.

"Paul was a wonderful guy. I was very lucky to play for him. I felt Paul was a god, to tell you the truth. He absolutely knew more about the game of baseball than any manager I ever played for. He knew what made each position tick. He just was a real student of the game.

"He was a little strange. I got to know him better probably after I retired and started doing games on television. I used to see him down in Texas when he was doing some scouting for Texas or was the assistant general manager, or advisor or whatever. He was a wonderful guy. But he might get on the elevator with you one day, coming down from the hotel where you were staying, and he wouldn't even acknowledge you. It was just like he was in another world. That's just the way he operated. But I'll tell you what—he was just terrific. We went to Arizona my first spring training. It was '56, although I played right out of high school in '55 in the minor leagues, and I played the last two weeks in Baltimore when I was 18. But we went out to Arizona the next year, Scottsdale, and we were there for '56, '57, and '58—three years, I believe. It was a great spring training camp. And I'll tell you what. We got to the ballpark at 10 o'clock in the morning, you'd work out, you'd do everything you had to do, then you'd play a game, and then you'd come back and work out in the afternoon. That's just the way he operated.

"Poor guys like Harry Brecheen and Luman Harris and Al Vincent [Richards' coaches], they were right out there with us the whole time. We just spent a lot of time at the ballpark, working on a lot of different things. But Paul was the greatest, really. He knew more about the game than anyone I ever knew. He was just like a foot above everyone else—the coaches, the managers. And there was no doubt who was in charge when Paul was there."

Richards was great at reclamation projects, turning mediocre pitchers into effective ones. And in part, Robinson says, Richards got the most out of his players through his intimidating manner.

"He also was wonderful at resurrecting careers, guys like Billy Loes. We had a whole handful of guys who came over to Baltimore, and they just became better pitchers when Paul got a hold of them. Really, that was his forte, I think, pitching more than anything else. We put in a lot of time, and I look back at it now, and that was really the way you had to do it then."

Part of Richards' genius was in evaluating talent. When Robinson first worked out before Richards after the Orioles had signed him out of Little Rock, he was a second baseman. Watching him work out at second base, Richards remarked to those around him that Robinson one day would be an All-Star third baseman, a prophetic baseball observation if there ever was one.

"Well, I played my first 50 games at second base in York, Pennsylvania, at Class B. And I guess [coach] George Staller and Paul got together and said, 'In the long run, we like this guy better at third base. He can catch the ball.' It wasn't any big adjustment. I played second base my last two years of Legion ball, and they just felt in the long run I'd be better over there at third, because it's more of a reflex position. I never had the great speed, so they said that third base would be my position."

When Robinson first came up, he lost a lot of time to injuries. One of the most frightening was when he was running toward the third base seats at Memorial Stadium and fell through an open door in a wall in foul territory.

"I had a lot of injuries early in my career. There was a big retaining wall, the seats were up above it, and they had an opening where they put the tractor [for grooming the field]. And they had a little chicken wire fence there. It was just chicken wire. It was only about five feet tall. I went after a foul ball one day. And I tried to stop. I put my hands on that wire and went right through. I split five teeth right in two. I've still got a scar here on my chin, where I had about 12 stitches. And I spent the whole winter in the dentist's chair back in Little Rock getting my root canals and everything done. And I had a knee operation in '57. I hurt my knee in '56 sliding into a base, and I partially tore cartilage in a game against Washington about two weeks into the season in '57. It took me a while to get over that. And then I went out to Vancouver [the Orioles Triple-A farm club at the time], and I was playing, and I ripped my arm up on a hook on a fence. I was pretty lucky in that situation, because I ripped my arm up pretty good, but it never bothered me after that. But after that, after those minor injuries, I played about 97 percent of the games for about a 15-year stretch. So I was lucky."

Robinson won 16 Gold Gloves for his play at third base, but he was not the only great infielder the Orioles had during his years in Baltimore. He is particularly grateful that he had good targets to throw to at first base for most of his tenure with the Orioles.

"Those guys, you're talking about the best there is. Louie [Aparicio] is about as good as anyone who's ever played the game of baseball at shortstop. And Belanger the same way, defensively. How do you get any better than those guys? Of course, Davey [Johnson] won some Gold Gloves at second base, and I played with [Bobby] Grich for three or four years, and I'll tell you, Bobby Grich played second base for those three or four years better than anybody in the history of baseball. That's the way I look at it. He was just a tremendous player.

"Of course, Boog [Powell] never won a Gold Glove, but he was a terrific guy to throw to. He had good hands, a big target over there. He remembers every ball I ever threw in the dirt that he dug out. I always claimed that every time I threw one in the dirt and he dug it out, he'd come into the dugout and mark it on the wall. And after the season he'd always say, 'There's 24 bad throws I dug out.' But he was a terrific first baseman.

"And when [Jim] Gentile was there, he was a good first baseman to throw to. The only guy that was a tough first baseman to throw to was Bob Boyd. Little Bob Boyd, a left-handed hitter, you had to put it on the money to him, because he didn't move around that well. But big guys with good hands at first base—like Boog and Gentile—they can really help you out."

Robinson also enjoyed playing with the team's original eccentric—center fielder Jackie Brandt.

"One day Jackie went up to the plate and said, 'I'm going to look for a change-up,' on a certain pitch. He went up there, and here comes the change-up, and he took it. And everyone said, 'You went up there looking for the change-up. How come you took it?' And he said, 'It was high, I was looking for it low.' Jackie was a real character."

One of the toughest decisions facing any major league baseball player, particularly a great one, is when to call it quits. Players generally do not recognize the ebbing of their talent with age as quickly as others do. Robinson tried to hang on as long as he could.

"I probably played longer than I should have. There's no doubt about it. But you always think you can play. You always think you can make some adjustments and you're ready to keep playing. I always thought it would be terrible to retire. I said they'd have to tear the uniform off me. But it really wasn't like that. In '77 the Orioles had told me that I could make my own deal and do what I wanted to, because I wasn't going to play much, unless Doug DeCinces got hurt. So I had talked to Seattle and Toronto, which were two new teams—Lou Gorman with Seattle and Pat Gillick at Toronto. I called them and said, 'Hey, I think I can still play some. I could help the organization.' I was ready to go somewhere. I had talked to my wife. But I never got a return call from them. That's just kind of the way baseball operates. You call people, and they never call back. It happens to all these guys.

Nobody ever returns calls in this business. That's just the way it is. All someone needs to do is call back and say, 'We don't need anyone, I'm sorry.' But that's not the way baseball operates.

"Anyhow, I came back in '77 after not doing well at all in either '75 or '76. I thought it was going to be a big transition. I was sitting that year, not doing much, taking batting practice, doing a little pinch hitting, played a game every now and then. And I just lost interest in the game. I was ready to hang them up, go out and get on with my life. And that was kind of the way it was. It wasn't really any big deal, when I retired."

CHAPTER 6

The Rope:
Bob Boyd
(1956-1960)

Bob Boyd was one of the first African Americans to play in the major leagues. A left-handed-hitting first baseman, he joined the Orioles in 1956 after several seasons with the White Sox. Boyd immediately became one of the team's best hitters. He batted over .300 in four of his five seasons in Baltimore, and his .318 average in 1957 remained the 10th highest in Orioles history through the 2003 season.

Boyd was a contact hitter who had little power. His career high for home runs in a season was seven in 1958. But he was one of the toughest men in the American League to strike out. As the team's regular first baseman, he never fanned more than 31 times in a season. The balls he hit were usually line-drive rockets. And those line-drive smashes gave birth to the nickname he earned as an Oriole: "The Rope."

"I wasn't a home run hitter. I was a line-drive hitter. One of our coaches, Luman Harris, was pitching batting practice to me one day, and I kept hitting line drives off him. So he pulled a rope from his pocket, and he showed it to me. And he said that's how I hit the ball, so he started calling me El Ropo, or The Rope."

While many hitters, especially those with a home run swing, found Memorial Stadium an onerous park to hit in, the old field on 33rd Street and its deep power alleys meshed perfectly with Boyd and his line-drive-laden bat.

"Memorial Stadium did me just fine. I hit to all the fields. And it was a pretty large stadium, so it suited me just fine. I had some pretty good years when I was with Baltimore, and I got to play."

Boyd says he never received much harassment because of his race while he was in the major leagues, shortly after baseball was integrated, but there were some incidents.

"I didn't have any real problems. They'd call you names, like 'Nigger' or 'Black.' But that was all right. I didn't pay it any mind. You couldn't live in some of the same hotels as the [white] players, in Kansas City, Missouri, St. Louis, Missouri, and Washington, D.C. They put us up in Negro hotels. It didn't make me feel bad. You just had to do the job.

"I didn't have any problems in the major leagues, not at all, not at all. I had a little problem when I was in the minor leagues, but I didn't pay it any mind."

One day in Yankee Stadium a fan tossed a bottle at him, but it wasn't because of his race. It was because of his bat.

"I broke up a no-hitter against the Yankees. We lost the game, but I got a line-drive double. After the third out that inning, I came back to the dugout and a fan threw a Coca-Cola bottle at me, and it hit me on the leg. He threw it because I broke up the no-hitter. I don't even remember who the pitcher was."

Back when Boyd played, before the major leagues had clubs on the West coast, the teams traveled from city to city by train. Boyd, who was born in Mississippi in 1926, preferred it that way.

"I loved traveling by train. You played cards, you'd read, you'd talk with the other players. It was real nice by train. But then we started flying. I never liked flying."

Bob Boyd. *Baltimore Orioles Photos*

CHAPTER 7

Sixteen Innings Later, A Victor:
Jerry Walker
(1957-1960)

The Orioles have had some wonderful pitchers and some beautifully pitched games over the years. Five no-hitters, 32 one-hitters, several hundred shutouts. But no Oriole ever pitched a more remarkable game than right-hander Jerry Walker on the night of September 11, 1959, against the Chicago White Sox.

"We played the White Sox an extremely high number of innings that year. We were both teams that had good pitching and good defense and didn't score a lot of runs. Of course the White Sox won the American League pennant that year. We played them [in] a lot of extra innings. I think we played them the equivalent of five extra games over the course of the season, in extra innings. I was in about four of those games.

"We played a doubleheader [one] night, and the double-header was necessitated because we had played an 18-inning, one-to-one tie. And, of course, it had to be started completely over. So we played the White Sox a doubleheader that night. Jack Fisher pitched the first game and pitched a 3-0 shutout. In the second game I started. The game was 0-0 going to the eighth or

Jerry Walker. *Baltimore Orioles Photos*

ninth inning, and [Paul] Richards asked how I was feeling, and I said, 'Fine.' I think I'd given up two or three hits at that point. So he said, 'I'm going to let you stay in the game.' So I stayed in the game, and in the 12th inning, I still was in the game. And it came to the 15th inning, and of course they had checked with me every inning to see how I was doing. So when it came to the 15th, they asked how I was feeling, and, again, I said, 'I'm fine.' So they let me go out in the 16th inning. When I came in, they said, 'That's it.' Fortunately, Brooks got a base hit in the bottom of the 16th inning [to put us ahead], 1-0. So I got the win. It was quite exciting. And people since then have pointed back and said, 'Well, that's where you hurt your arm.' I can't say that I did, and I can't say that I didn't. The next year I was not as effective. I had some physical problems, allergies and so forth. And all of our young pitchers came up that year and were pitching well whenever I got out of the rotation. I didn't really pitch a lot after that. I actually hurt my arm for the first time with Kansas City two years later, in 1961.

"I don't think you're going to see anybody pitching 16 innings now, for more reasons than one. There's an extreme amount of care taken to watch pitch counts, that kind of stuff. In terms of pitch counts, I threw a lot of pitches. But for 16 innings, it was not a lot. I think it was in the 170 range, or something like that, which is about 11 pitches an inning. If a guy pitches a complete game with 11 pitches an inning, that's 99 pitches. That's nothing. Look what happened in the years after that, when the Nolan Ryans of the world came along, and threw 150-200 pitches every time [they] went out, most of the time on three days' rest. It's kind of what you condition yourself to, but certainly the game has changed. Now, with relief pitching the way it is, a guy can be pitching a shutout and it gets to the ninth inning, and a team has a dominant closer, he can be pitching the ninth inning.

"I was just trying to win a ball game that night, and I didn't really think about the number of innings that I was pitching. It was not common then for someone to go out and throw 15 or 16 innings. But I was pitching well, we weren't scoring and they weren't scoring, and he let me stay in the game. I was extremely sore the next day, but I think anyone would be after doing something like that, which they weren't accustomed to.

"During the game, I was fine. I had thrown several games. I was 20 years old. They watched what I did. I started and relieved. If I relieved between starts, they would push me back a couple of days and give me my full rest before I pitched again. I would guess in my top game I would throw in the 130-135 range. So this game was more, but certainly not an extreme amount."

Walker's bat was almost as strong as his arm that night. He got two hits in the game and allowed the Sox only six over his 16 innings. The game took three hours and 40 minutes, not long for 16 innings by today's standards, but almost twice as long as Fisher's shutout in the first game. The contest was wrapped up in a tidy one hour and 45 minutes.

Walker, now a front office executive with the St. Louis Cardinals, was one of the Orioles' famed bonus babies of the 1950s. It seems ludicrous now, but at the time, the signing of a young player for $4,000 or more was considered extravagant. So much so, in fact, it was discouraged by a rule that required a team to keep bonus babies on the major-league roster for at least two years, even though they had no minor-league experience.

"I was a bonus baby because I got over $4,000, so I had to stay on the major-league club for two years. I signed in June or July of '57 and spent the rest of that year there. Then they did away with the rule and made it retroactive, so I didn't have to stay with the team the next year.

"I went to my first spring training in Arizona in '58, and I think I pitched about 45 innings. I broke with the team out of spring training, but I had a little health problem so I didn't pitch the first three weeks. So Paul Richards said he wanted me to go out and pitch. So I went to Knoxville and spent that year there, and I was back [in Baltimore] at the end of the year.

"I remember sitting on the bench the first year I was up and Richards wanted someone to pinch hit. He got up and called the coach over and told him he wanted the guy sitting right next to him [Richards] to pinch hit, instead of saying it directly to that guy. I had no idea [that not] all major-league managers were like that. I thought he was a very sharp baseball man, stayed ahead of the game, knew what was happening, was not afraid to try something that he thought would help win a ball game."

CHAPTER 8

The Reluctant Cincinnati Kid:
Milt Pappas
(1957-1965)

Before there was a Cuellar, Flanagan or Mussina, there was Milt Pappas. From 1958 through 1965, when the Orioles were struggling to reach prominence, the right-hander from Detroit was arguably the club's top pitcher. Pappas won at least 10 games in each of those eight years and never had a losing season as a Baltimore starter. Although the Orioles developed a whole stable of great pitchers after Pappas last threw a ball for them, he remains among the top seven or better in team history in wins, strikeouts, shutouts and complete games.

Despite his obvious talents and outstanding performance as a pitcher in the Orioles' early days, however, Pappas probably is best remembered for being traded from the team. On December 9, 1965, the Orioles dealt Pappas (along with pitcher Jack Baldschun and outfielder Dick Simpson, neither of whom ever played a single inning for Baltimore) to Cincinnati for Frank Robinson. It was that deal, bringing Robinson to Memorial Stadium, that turned the Orioles into a world champion the next year and made them a major-league power for the next decade.

While the transaction proved to be a bonanza for the Orioles—perhaps the best deal in their history—it did not particularly please Pappas.

"I was not happy about the trade. On our last road trip of the 1965 season, we were coming back to Baltimore, and [starting pitcher] Steve Barber saw Lee MacPhail, the general manager, and Hank Bauer, the manager. He went up to them and said he hated Baltimore, he hated the team, and he hated the organization, and he wanted to be traded. So I thought if anyone would be traded in the off-season, it would be Steve Barber.

"I was down in Florida after the season. I was the Orioles player representative, and we had meetings down in Florida. I called my wife, because she was planning to come down to Florida in a few days to look for a house for us for spring training. She said there were a lot of trade rumors up in Baltimore. I said, 'Involving whom?' She said, 'You.'

"It so happened, that evening, as I was coming out of the hotel, Lee MacPhail and Hank Bauer were walking into the Fountainbleu Hotel. I walked up to them and said, 'Hey guys, I just talked to my wife, and she said there were a lot of trade rumors involving me.' They said, 'Oh no, you're not going to be traded, you're the best pitcher we've got.' That made me feel a whole lot better. A couple days later my wife came down. It was raining, and we went to see a movie. It was *The Cincinnati Kid.*

"Five days later, I got a call and was told I was traded to Cincinnati for Frank Robinson. I was devastated. And the following year, I was pitching for Cincinnati, mired in fifth place, and the Orioles went on to win the World Series. It was heartbreaking."

Most of Pappas' career with the Orioles, however, was far from heartbreaking. He was a winning pitcher when the club was still losing most of its games. And one of his most rewarding wins came against the team that ruled baseball during Pappas' years in Baltimore—the New York Yankees.

"Back then, the Yankees were the most dominating team, with the likes of Mickey Mantle, Yogi Berra, Bill Skowron and Whitey Ford. It just seemed in the American League like we were always fighting for second place. First place belonged to the Yankees.

Milt Pappas. *Brace Photo*

"The Yankees came into Baltimore for a three-game set. The Yankees won the first two at Memorial Stadium. They really kicked the hell out of us. We were fighting for the pennant that year. John Steadman, the Baltimore baseball writer, came up to me. I just wanted to get the hell out of there, but John came up to me and said, 'Milt, how the heck do you beat this team?' And I said, 'It was a very simple equation to beat the Yankees. You shut them out and hit a home run to win the game.' The next afternoon he wrote those words that I had told him in the newspaper. And then, that night, I shut them out and hit a home run to beat the Yankees, 1-0. I made John look like a prophet. Any time you beat the Yankees back then, though, it was a great feeling."

Pappas had an unusual experience on August 28, 1960, giving up what he thought was a game-losing home run against the White Sox, only to have it called back by an umpire.

"It was the top of the eighth inning, and we were winning, 3-1, and Ted Kluszewski was up. There were two men on base. I threw a pitch and Kluszewski hit it out of the ballpark. So we went from a 3-1 lead to a 4-3 deficit. But at the same time, Ed Hurley, the third base umpire, had called time out. I had thought I'd heard someone call time just as I was about to release the pitch, but I wasn't able to stop. And Ed Hurley had indeed called time out. It was kind of funny, because Hurley was the third base umpire, and the reason he called time was because of what was happening in the White Sox bullpen, all the way on the other side of the field. He felt the White Sox pitcher and catcher weren't in the right position as they were warming up in the bullpen. Al Lopez [the White Sox manager] went completely crazy. He went absolutely berserk. And after everything was restored, and everybody got back to near normalcy, I actually threw Kluszewski the same pitch, and he popped it up. So we ended up winning, 3-1."

CHAPTER 9

The Flake:
Jackie Brandt
(1960-1965)

Jackie Brandt was one of the most colorful—and, at least to his managers, maddening—players ever to wear an Orioles uniform. A native of Nebraska, he played center-field for Baltimore from 1960 to 1965. Brandt came from the San Francisco Giants with glowing reviews, but he never quite lived up to his potential. Club officials believed his eccentricities prevented him from allowing his raw baseball talent to fully flourish. Brandt usually said and did whatever was on his mind. He earned the nickname "Flake," a sobriquet he wore as proudly as he did his major league uniform.

One of the more famous stories involving Brandt was an ice cream outing he cajoled other players into taking with him when the team was in New York to play the Yankees. Brandt has told the story many times and insists it's true. Others say it is Apocrypha. But whether genuine or not, it has become part of the Brandt legend.

"We were in New York City. And if you stayed in a hotel in New York then, all they ever had as far as ice cream is concerned was chocolate, strawberry and vanilla. I didn't want one of those three. I wanted something different. So I got a couple of my buddies on the team, and we took a cab out of the city. There was nothing to get then in New York for a different kind of ice cream. We went about 20 or 30 miles in the cab, to some place like Dobbs Ferry. They had an ice cream place there, like a Baskin Robbins. The problem was, though, that they had so many flavors, I didn't know what to take. So I took a vanilla cone."

That was vintage Brandt—being the oddball, taking a cab an hour out of New York City to get a more exotic ice cream flavor and then ending up with a simple vanilla cone. But it wasn't only his antics that raised attention—and bewilderment—but also his words.

"One day, it was the last game of the season, the general manager, Lee MacPhail, was making the rounds in the clubhouse. He came up to me and said, 'Have a nice winter, Jackie.' I said, 'I always have nice winters. It's the damn summers that kill me.' A lot of goofy stuff came out of me when I was with the Orioles. I never knew what was going to come out."

Brandt lived just two blocks from Memorial Stadium and used to walk to the park.

"We never had many fans back then. Things have changed now. I used to do a lot of different things then. But I think all of the other players were odd and eccentric. I was the only normal one in the group."

It would be hard to convince his one-time manager, no-nonsense ex-Marine Hank Bauer, that Brandt was the sane one on the club.

"One day we were taking batting practice in Washington. Charlie Lau was our backup catcher. He was pitching batting practice for about 20 minutes that day. I hit about seven balls in a row into the bullpen beyond the left-field fence. The manager, Hank Bauer, was by the cage, and he said to me, 'Why don't you do that in the game?' I said, 'Put Lau out there to pitch against me, and I will.' Everybody laughed, but not the manager. Bauer didn't like me too much. And after everybody laughed at what I had said that day, he didn't play me that game."

Sometimes Brandt would even carry his offbeat behavior into a ball game.

Jackie Brandt. *Baltimore Orioles Photos*

"In the minor leagues one day, the other team had the bases loaded with two outs in the ninth, and we're one run ahead. Their little second baseman was at bat, and he didn't have much power. So I moved in from the outfield and played on the dirt right behind second base. No one really even noticed. And the little second baseman, he hit a line drive right to me. It would have been a single if I hadn't been there. I just had a gut feeling. I was pretty good at that. I guess that's why they called me flakey."

Then there was the time the Orioles were playing in Washington when Brandt flummoxed everyone, even, apparently, the umpires.

"We were playing another game in Washington, the bases were loaded, and we're one or two ahead. Stu Miller is pitching in the ninth inning. I creep up toward the infield. The guy hits a blooper to the outfield. I run in and catch it on the trap. I went in to second base with the ball. All the time running in, I'm talking to Luis Aparicio, who's playing short, and Jerry Adair, who was at second. I didn't want to give the ball to nobody. I said if I step on second base then there's just one out. If I touch the guy who's off second first, I can get a double play. So I reached over and touched the guy and then put my foot on the base. Then I dropped the ball and ran to the dugout. But the umpire said everyone was safe. And we ended up losing the ball game by one run. After the game I said I knew what I did was right. And I was going to tell the reporters what I did, and tell them that the umpire had blown the call. But the manager came over to me and said, 'Say "No comment." If you try to explain what happened, the umpire will get us back the next game.' So I was under orders not to defend myself. I had to say 'No comment.' And the next day the paper said Brandt's nutty play lost the Orioles the game."

CHAPTER 10

The Diamond in the Rough:
Jim Gentile
(1960-1963)

J im Gentile was one of the most colorful and volatile
players—both in temperament and with his bat—ever
to wear an Orioles uniform. He was a strapping 6-foot-4
first baseman with a classical stretch from the bag, his long
legs splitting horizontally along the infield dirt as he gracefully
gobbled up errant throws from his infielders. But Gentile was
known for his bat, not his glove. He put together what for many
years was the best offensive season ever by an Orioles hitter in
1961—a .302 average with 46 home runs and 141 RBIs. Manager
Paul Richards didn't play Gentile against tough lefties, but his
home-run percentage in 1961 just barely trailed that of Roger
Maris and Mickey Mantle. He never got as much credit as he
deserved in 1961. Maris was chasing and breaking Babe Ruth's
home-run record, and another first baseman, Norm Cash of the
Tigers, batted a league-high .361. Gentile didn't even make the
All-Star team.

If ever a player had a classic baseball nickname, it was the
Orioles' "Diamond Jim" Gentile.

"Roy Campanella hung the name 'Diamond Jim,' on me in 1956 when I was with the Dodgers organization. I went to Japan with the team. I'd played at Fort Worth and hit 40 home runs there that year, and the Dodgers took me and Don Demeter along. I was just hitting everything when we were over there. I was leading the team in home runs and batting average. The military newspaper, *The Stars and Stripes*, asked Campanella what he thought of this young Italian kid named Gentile, and Campanella said, 'He's a diamond in the rough.'

"In 1961 when I was with the Orioles, we went into Minnesota. The clubhouse guy there was the same one I'd had in St. Paul in 1959. He put up a sign that said, 'Welcome home, Diamond Jim.' Then I went out and hit two grand slams there in one game. When I was in the minors, they didn't call me Diamond Jim, but they used it when I got called up to the big leagues."

That two-grand slam day was one of the mightiest offensive performances ever by an Oriole. Gentile picked up nine RBIs for his day's work. Chuck Estrada was on the mound for the Orioles that day, earning the 13-5 win. But that was no surprise. Gentile hit five grand slams in 1961, and in each game that he cleared the bases with a homer, Estrada was the Orioles' starting pitcher.

The day in Minnesota when he knocked two out of the park was the grandest of them all. He hit grand slams in both the first and second innings, becoming the first player in baseball history to hit grand slams in consecutive at-bats.

"I hit the two grand slams on May 9, 1961. My memories are wonderful of that day. When you do something like that, you don't realize at the time what you've done. After the second one, when I crossed the plate, Paul Richards hit me on my rear and said, 'Son, I don't think that's ever been done before.' Back then, managers didn't talk to you unless they were going to release you. Back in Memorial Stadium, you almost had to raise your hand to go to the bathroom from the dugout. You could be sitting right next to Richards, and he'd turn to [coach] Luman [Harris] and say, 'Luman, get Diamond up to hit.' He wouldn't talk directly to you."

Gentile almost didn't make it with the Orioles when they acquired him the previous year from the Dodgers. Had it not

Jim Gentile. *Baltimore Orioles Photos*

been for Richards' uncanny ability to judge baseball talent, Gentile might never have worn an Orioles uniform.

"I went to the Orioles in 1960 for $50,000 and two players, Willie Miranda and Bill Lajoie. Part of the deal was that if I didn't make the club out of spring training, they'd send me back to the Dodgers. They already had Walt Dropo and Bob Boyd to play first, and Boog was there that spring, too. I had just a terrible spring training. I didn't do anything right. And one day, Whitey Driscoll, the Orioles' clubhouse guy, told me to go in to see Richards. The night before Sparky Anderson had talked to me. He was managing at [AAA] Toronto. He told me the Dodgers were expecting to get a hard-hitting first baseman back. And Sparky asked me if I'd come to Toronto. I said yes, because I'd played eight years in the minors at that point. But when I went in to see Richards, he said, 'Son, you can't be as bad as you look. I looked at your minor league record, and it's great. And all you have is 36 at-bats with the Dodgers in three years.' He said, 'I'm going to give you 150 at-bats. If you hit, you're my first baseman. If not, on the 30th day, you'll be back with the Dodgers.'

"We opened the season at home in Baltimore, and all of the local sports writers were really surprised when he played me. I went one-for-four and made two first-to-home double plays in the field. The next day I got three hits and two home runs against Camilo Pascual of Washington, and that was the beginning. Through all of 1960 I played against right-handers. I hit 21 home runs and got 98 RBIs. I had 98 RBIs with three games left. The writers said I'd get Rookie of the Year if I got 100 RBIs, but I only played one game and didn't get the 100 RBIs. The Rookie of the Year was our shortstop in Baltimore, Ron Hansen."

Regardless of what he did or how well he played, Gentile never seemed to be satisfied. His temper was as big as his body, and teammates became used to his outbursts when he failed to achieve what he set out to do.

"Gus Triandos came up to me after '61 and said, 'Diamond, you had a year anyone would die for, and you were pissed off all year.'"

CHAPTER 11

A Lust for Life:
Boog Powell
(1961-1974)

Boog Powell is the Paul Bunyan of Baltimore baseball, a legendary giant of a man who carried a big club and had a thirst for life and baseball as large as his girth and his appetite for pit barbecue. No one ever needed to use his last name when speaking of him, nor did many people even know his given name, John Wesley Powell. It was just Boog.

Powell was just a teenager when the Orioles invited him to major-league spring training camp and offered him what he thought was a legitimate chance to make the Baltimore roster in 1960.

"We were in spring training the year before I came up. I had had a wonderful spring, and [Jim] Gentile had come over from the Dodgers. I think I hit .380 or something that spring. I was just tearing it up. I was working real hard. I was just 18 years old. I thought that maybe I was ready for the big leagues, because I was hitting big-league pitching down in spring training, and I was playing every day. I thought, 'This doesn't seem that difficult. This is pretty easy.'

"But Paul Richards called me into his office, and he said, 'Son, we're going to send you out.' So I went from almost making the club to going to Class B ball. And he says, 'I know you've worked really hard this spring, why don't you go back down to Key West'—I was living in Key West—'and take some time off?' I said, 'What do you mean, take some time off?' He said, 'Just take a week off. And report to Earl Weaver in Thomasville when you feel like it sometime next week. They're not due to break camp until next week.' I said to myself, 'Well, maybe this is the way they do it.'

"So I took off, and I went home. I went down to Key West. I was sitting down there, and I said, 'What in the hell am I doing here? This is stupid. I'm a ball player. I'm going to get my ass out of here.' So I took off, and I drove to Thomasville. I drove all night. When I got there I was No. 540-something. I had No. 540 on my back. You stayed in barracks, it was an army base, and the field where you played was a little over a mile away. So you got up in the morning, and you had breakfast, and then you had to run to the damn field. Of course, we'd been out chasing all the local girls at night. The only thing you had going in those days was the local pizza parlor. And you'd end up pissing off all the local guys because you'd be trying to chase their girls around. But that was Thomasville."

Powell was not that upset that he didn't make the team in 1960. He just was happy to be playing professional baseball, even if it was in the minor leagues.

"I didn't care. I really didn't. You know, I cared, but I was playing ball, and I'd been in the rookie league the year before, and I wasn't sure what to expect when I got to Thomasville. Of course there were all these guys there like Dave Nicholson, the Orioles' big bonus baby. He was there. And so were Bo Belinski and Dean Chance. The Orioles had a lot of prospects back in those days. We lost them, of course, in that [expansion] draft."

Eventually, more than a year later and with some Triple-A experience under his spikes, Powell got the call to the big time.

"I'd had a good year in Rochester, and they called me up when the team was in Yankee Stadium. That was in '61, and I think

Boog Powell. *Baltimore Orioles Photos*

Maris had 57 or 58 [home runs] at the time. And I come into town, and Paul Richards had just stepped down [as manager], and Luman Harris had taken over the club. Luman came up to me that day, and he said, 'You're playing left field.' I said, 'You know, I haven't played left field but once all year. In Rochester I played first base every day.' And he says, 'You're my starting left fielder.' He says, 'You better get your ass out there [in batting practice] and start catching some fly balls.' So I went out there, and I started catching some fly balls.

"Of course, there were 75,000 people in Yankee Stadium. There were white shirts everywhere. There's more people in Yankee Stadium than there is in my hometown—that one night. I come from Lakeland, Florida. There's 25,000 people in my hometown, and there's 75,000 people in that damn ballpark. I'm going, 'Damn.' I didn't have any of my bats. None of my stuff made it to the ballpark. I'd come off a big year. I'd hit .320 or so and hit 30 home runs in Triple-A. I really felt good. But in my first at-bat, when I walked to the plate, I can barely remember it. I mean my knees were shaking so bad, I was almost out of control. I wasn't scared, but I was just…I don't know, maybe I was scared. I struck out—miserably. They could have thrown anything. They could have not even thrown the ball, and I would have swung. They could have just gone out there and gone through the motions like they were pitching.

"Then all of a sudden, after that, I was okay. In the next at-bat, I got a base hit and ended up driving in the winning run in that ball game. It was a big thrill. The story I like to tell all the time is that before the game, Luman Harris came up to me and said, 'You're not nervous, are you?' And I said, 'No, I'm not nervous at all.' So he says, 'Well, you know, kid, up here in the big leagues we wear our supporter on the inside.'"

Powell was a very accomplished hitter, and he rattled many big-league pitchers with the artistry of his bat. One of the hurlers he pestered the most was the great and stylish Cuban pitcher, Luis Tiant.

"I think El Tiante had something like 23 or 24 consecutive scoreless innings, and we were facing them over there in Cleveland. He threw me a pitch up and in, and I just turned on it. I really got jammed on the pitch, and I hit it out to left center, and it went out. There was a guy on, and it broke up his scoreless-innings streak. He was looking at me all the way around the bases. The next day, in the Cleveland paper, he was saying how lucky I was and that I could never hit that pitch again in 100 years. All of a sudden, something clicked, and I never figured it out, but I just started hitting him so good. It didn't matter, all of that motion that he had, and all of that stuff, I just saw right through it all. It was like I was on a different page. I don't know exactly what my numbers were against him, but I just wore his ass out. Years later we were doing some Miller Lite commercials together, traveling around the country working for the Miller Brewing Company. And he'd say, 'Hey man, how come you were so hard on me? You killed me, man, you killed me.' And I said, 'Luis, I was just lucky, man.' But I wish I could have figured out how I could have bottled that concentration that I had when I was facing him after the statement that he had made about how lucky I was to hit that home run. I never really quite figured it out. I have never had that feeling against anyone else. I hit some guys pretty good, but with him, it was like, 'I don't care what you throw, I'm going to be on it. It doesn't matter what you throw, I'm going to be all over you.'

"And he was frustrated. He really was. I hit some balls off him that were just monster home runs. Over the exit in Cleveland down the right-field line, I hit one that hit the back of the façade on the upper deck, way up there. It was dark up there, and the ball just sort of disappeared way up there. I thought, 'How do you like that one?' I wasn't real mad at him or anything; it was just like I'd gone to another level."

Despite his size, Powell was graceful with the glove at first. He also appreciated the fact that he played in an infield that included some of the best defensive wizards in the game.

"What a treat it was playing across the infield from Brooks. And for years I played behind Brooks in left field. I used to break on balls out there, but we had Aparicio at short and Brooksie over at third, and nothing ever came through. I hardly ever got any ground balls in left field unless they were line drives.

"And then I got the opportunity to go to first base and to see Brooks firsthand and just marvel at how great he was—to watch the things that he did day in and day out. Of course the 1970 World Series was a showcase for him. If he would have played in New York, they would have seen that all the time because he did that every day. He made those kinds of plays every day. I mean what he did in the 1970 World Series was just normal kinds of plays for him. Of course, we kidded all the time about what a great half a play that was. Every one of those plays was a ball [thrown to first] in the dirt, and if I missed it, it was just E-5, that's all it is. It's no big deal. Brooksie made an error. So he ends up getting the car from *Sport Magazine*, a little Corvette or something like that. And I just told him, 'If I don't catch those balls, I probably win it. So I want half that car, half the Corvette.' We just laughed about it. We still laugh a lot about it."

Powell was not only a prodigious batsman, but he also was a prodigious denizen of the night. He liked having a good time, both on and off the field. Many players couldn't keep up with Powell at night. He was able to party and play baseball at the same time. And one of his best days ever on a baseball diamond followed quickly on the heels of a late evening—or really an early morning—of partying.

"Steve Barber had pitched a really good game on a Saturday night in July. Kansas City was in town, and we went out to dinner after the game with his wife and my wife. Then I invited them back to our house, and we sat around down in my rec room, and we talked until four o'clock in the morning, or so. Then we showed up at the ballpark for a doubleheader on Sunday—the next day. It turns out, the first at-bat—Alvin Dark was managing Kansas City—the bases were loaded in the first inning, and I come up. I can't remember who was pitching, but it was a left-hander, and I bailed out, and I did a little checked swing flare down the left-field line. It cleared the bases, and I ended up with a triple. Alvin Dark was screaming when I came back out to first base in the next inning. He's screaming, there again, about how lucky I was. He's yelling this and that, and 'Swing the bat like a grown man.' Blah. Blah. Blah. Blah. So, I said, 'Okay.' Then the next time up I hit one by the first baseman, just a bullet. I mean right down the line. And then I hit a three-run homer.

"Anyway, to make a long story short, I drove in 11 runs that day. I hit three home runs, got like seven hits on the whole day. And I felt really bad, from the night before. We ended up losing one of those games, we lost the second game. But I had hit a home run to tie it up. In the bottom of the ninth, I hit a two-run home run off Jack Aker to tie it up. I can remember saying, 'If I could do that every night…' And Alvin Dark never said a word to me, and I never talked to him after that. We never crossed paths, and he was nowhere to be found after about the fifth at-bat. I hit a grand slam off Wes Stock and a three-run homer off someone else. And he was all over me. Alvin was kind of a religious man, and he didn't usually say too much, but, boy, he was all over me that day, and it just struck me wrong. Maybe if more of those things would have happened, I might be in the Hall of Fame."

CHAPTER 12

The Turkey:
Dick Hall
(1961-1966; 1969-1971)

Before relief pitchers—and closers in particular—were considered essential parts of a big-league roster, Dick Hall served in those roles for the Orioles and was a key player on the club's early championship teams. He'd come in late in a game if a starter got in trouble. Sometimes he'd pitch one inning, sometimes two or three. If he was pitching well in a game, his manager might keep him in until the game ended. In a sense, he was both a short-man and a closer.

Hall was tall and lean, and his arms and legs seemed to fly every which way when he released the ball. He stood 6-foot-6 but weighed only 200 pounds. Hall looked like the Disney cartoon character Gyro Gearloose on the mound. Because of his long and spindly arms and legs, and the way he pitched, his teammates called him Turkey. A *Washington Post* sports writer once described his pitching form as akin to "a drunken giraffe on roller skates."

"I was the tallest Oriole for a while. They grow them bigger now. I had a herky-jerky motion. I led with my elbow. I couldn't help the way I pitched, but it worked. My release point was almost like sidearm, but it was close to my body. I threw like a girl, kind

Dick Hall. *Baltimore Orioles Photos*

of, with the elbow first, sort of a three-quarters delivery, with the arm tucked in. People sometimes described it as sidearm, but it really wasn't."

The manner in which Hall threw a baseball was not the only way he differed from other pitchers. He was a graduate of Swarthmore, a liberal arts school more noted for producing scholars than athletes. During his playing career, Hall became an accountant, a profession he actually worked in during the off-season and long after his retirement from the playing field in 1971. He also began his career as an outfielder, not as a pitcher.

Despite the fact that he was the rare major leaguer to come from the Swarthmore campus, Hall believes the fact that he attended the school helped him win a big-league contract.

"I signed with Pittsburgh in 1952. Branch Rickey was with the Pirates then, and one of his daughters went to Swarthmore. And two of his daughters married fraternity brothers of mine. I think I might have been Rickey's pet, in a sense. I was from a school that he sent his daughter to. I think I was fortunate in that way. I signed a bonus, not really a big one, and I think that helped my career.

"I played in the outfield in the Blackstone Valley League [in Pennsylvania]. And when I played semi-pro, and all through college, I pitched. I didn't play the outfield. But most clubs wanted to sign me as a position player, so Rickey did that. I even got a shot with the Pirates, platooning in the outfield with Jerry Lynch in Pittsburgh."

In 1954, his first regular season with Pittsburgh, Hall hit .239 with two home runs as an outfielder. He never threw a pitch. But that would change by the next season.

"I played winter ball in Mexico and told my manager that I had pitched in college. I was on the team in Mazatlan, an archrival of Culican. One Sunday near the end of winter season, the starter got knocked out, and I was given the chance to pitch. I allowed three hits over six innings. It happened again, so I got another chance to pitch. One of the Pittsburgh scouts saw me. So next spring they tried me as pitcher. And I turned out to be a much better pitcher than a hitter."

For a time, Hall held the Mexican League's record for lowest ERA, as well as its record for most home runs in a season. He also met his wife in Mazatlan.

Hall always enjoyed hitting, and three times in his career as a pitcher, he batted over .300, though with a very limited number of at-bats. In 1963 for the Orioles, he went 13-for-28 (.464) with a home run. But it was from the mound that Hall truly made his mark as an Oriole. He was noted particularly for his amazing control.

"I pitched for 14 years and had only one wild pitch. I also have a really low walk-per-nine-innings record. My last seven seasons I gave up only 23 unintentional bases on balls. In my last six seasons I had more wins than unintentional walks. I'm curious where I stand on the all-time list for unintentional walks per nine innings.

"When I pitched, relief pitchers came in just when the starters got in trouble. Weaver wouldn't let the starter give up the winning run. Earl had my role down pat—I would come in the seventh inning in close games, or in extra innings. I'd normally pitch two or three innings at a time. At the beginning I was a starter, but I had some arm trouble, and when I got to Baltimore, they had a really good staff, so I switched to relief. I actually began in that role as a long reliever. As a short reliever, if I came in in the seventh, I'd finish the game if I didn't get into trouble, so I got a number of saves."

One of Hall's typically superlative performances came in 1961 in the first game he ever pitched in Yankee Stadium.

"The year before I was a starter with Kansas City, and we had a five-man rotation, but I never had pitched at Yankee Stadium. Paul Richards went with me as a closer that year. Milt Pappas was pitching in this game, and he had a one-run lead in the eighth. Starting the ninth, they didn't pinch hit for him. At the beginning of the Yankees' half of the ninth, Pappas had nothing. But Richards made up his mind that he was going to let Milt finish. He walked the bases loaded, and the fourth batter of the inning, Clete Boyer had two balls on him. Richards finally had enough.

"So I came in with the bases loaded, two balls and no strikes on Boyer, and no one out with a one-run lead. I struck out Boyer on a 3-2 pitch that was borderline, down low. Boyer was so mad that he broke his bat on the ground. Hector Lopez was the next batter up. He hit my first pitch on the ground to Ron Hansen at short, and as he did, he slipped in the batter's box. Talk about a tailor-made double play. Ralph Houk [the Yankees' manager] came out to argue after the game. And he got a suspension for it. So that was my first game in Yankee Stadium. It was one of my most memorable experiences."

Hall had another very memorable game at Yankee Stadium on September 20, 1961. It was the Yankees' 154th game of the season. Roger Maris was chasing Babe Ruth's home-run record of 60. Early in the game, Maris had hit number 59 off the Orioles' starter, Milt Pappas. Some baseball people believed for Maris to truly break Ruth's record he had to do so in 154 games. The season was lengthened to 162 games a few years earlier, but in Ruth's day, only 154 games were played.

"I faced Maris twice. I struck him out the first time, then he hit a shot at our right fielder. I also got a base hit in that game."

Maris' 1961 season more recently was made into a television movie, and the film included the game in which Hall pitched against him.

"I like to say, 'How many people had an actor play you in a movie?'"

Hall left the Orioles in 1966, but returned three years later.

"In the last half of '66 I had a bad arm. I was traded to Philadelphia for a player to be named later, and they didn't even bother to name the player until after the end of the next season."

Hall has the distinction of winning the first American League Champion Series game in history, beating the Twins in relief on October 4, 1969.

"I was the winning pitcher in the first [ALCS] playoff game ever. I came in with the bases loaded and one out, and got out of that inning. And we scored in the bottom half of the inning."

CHAPTER 13

Old Man:
Robin Roberts
(1962-1965)

Hall of Famer Robin Roberts was one of the National League's premier right-handers in the 1950s. Pitching for the Phillies, he had six consecutive 20-win seasons, highlighted by a 28-7 record in 1952. He won the honor of being the starting pitcher in the All-Star game five times—a record he shares with Lefty Gomez and Don Drysdale.

But by the end of the '50s, his relationship with the Phillies began to sour, and they released him after the 1961 season. He had a spring training tryout with the Yankees in 1962, but the Bronx Bombers passed on Roberts. The Orioles stepped into the gap and signed him. Roberts went on to win 42 games for Baltimore over the next four years as one of the club's top starters. And on Sunday, August 26, 1962, five months after the Yankees chose not to sign him, Roberts made New York regret that decision.

"We had just had two doubleheaders with the Yankees on Friday and Saturday. And we had won all four of those games. Then we had a single game on Sunday, and Whitey [Ford] was pitching for the Yankees. I pitched for the Orioles. I was with the Yankees that spring, but they released me after one week. I never pitched for them.

"In the game against Whitey, Tony Kubek hit a home run off me early. And in the fourth inning, Brooksie hit a home run for us. And then Jim Gentile, who hadn't had a lot of success against Whitey, hit one [out]. Then after those three solo home runs, the game settled down. We won the game, 2-1, and I pitched a complete-game five-hitter. It was exciting for me, and it was exciting for the team, winning five in a row over the Yankees.

"The Yankees had picked me up on waivers in December. It hadn't been working out for me with the Phillies. We weren't a good ball club, and I'd had a bad year. It made sense for me to go. Probably I should have left earlier. It was disappointing to be dropped by the Yankees. I just didn't know after they released me what I was going to do. I had conversations with a couple of teams, and the Orioles invited me to work out with them after I called them.

"So beating the Yankees anytime felt good. It was especially nice to beat a pitcher like Whitey. And winning five straight was great for the team and for me, personally. There wasn't much excitement overall for the team that year. We weren't that good. 1963 was better, and in 1964 we held the lead going into September. The 1964 team was one of the better clubs I ever played for. I thought we had a good chance to win the pennant. Brooksie had a big year, the best year I've seen from a teammate. He not only fielded well, but he hit well, too. And he won the league MVP award.

"The pitching staff in those years was great. Milt Pappas was a much better pitcher than people realized. He could really get batters out. But he'd pull himself out of games. Today that's an accepted practice. Milt was just before his time. It didn't happen much then, for a pitcher to pull himself out, especially when you were pitching well and had the lead. But he had this tendency to take himself out, and that detracted from his reputation.

"Skinny Brown and Hoyt Wilhelm also were with the Orioles when I was there. And Gus Triandos. But that's about it. The rest of the guys were much younger than I was. I enjoyed watching the

Robin Roberts. *Baltimore Orioles Photos*

young players. I saw Dave McNally develop into a fine pitcher. And Steve Barber was a tremendous pitcher. He had great stuff, and he really made guys look silly at the plate. I think he hurt his arm, because he never developed fully. Wally Bunker also had a good year [in 1965]. He won 19 games. He just sort of snuck up on people. He could really throw when I was there.

"I was just so happy to be pitching when I was with the Orioles that nothing bothered me. A lot of the young players called me 'Old Man'. And when we went on road trips, I'd hang around with [broadcaster] Chuck Thompson and the other announcers. They were more my age.

"I roomed with Jim Palmer. We were out in Los Angeles, and one night he said, 'Tell me about pitching.' I just said, 'Throw the hell out of the ball, and now go to sleep.' He said that was some of the best advice he ever got."

CHAPTER 14

A Character Actor:
Bob Johnson
(1963-1967)

B
ob Johnson was the Orioles' version of a character
actor. He was a role player, and an important one on
the mid-1960s teams. Johnson played five full seasons
in Baltimore but never had more than 273 at-bats in any year.
He primarily served as a utility infielder and pinch hitter. It was
in the latter role that he gained some fleeting fame. He's one of
11 Johnsons to have played for the Orioles but the only one who
once held an American League pinch-hitting record.

"I was privileged to be part of the World Series team in '66,
although I didn't get in a game. I was one of the 12 who didn't
play one inning, or even one-half inning. We had 25 players
eligible and only 13 played. We never used a pinch hitter, never
used a pinch runner, and only used four pitchers. It was the largest
unemployment check I ever received.

"I was fortunate to set an American League pinch-hit record
with six consecutive pinch hits in 1964, which lasted until 1981,
when Bill Stein broke that record. The thing that's kind of unusual
about that is when he broke it, they had the designated-hitter
rule. They didn't have it when I was playing, which meant that

maybe they wouldn't have to pinch hit as often, that whoever he was pinch hitting for was a regular. I had eight consecutive hits at one time, which tied an Orioles record. I'm not sure if that exists or not [it no longer does].

"The sixth consecutive pinch hit was a big thrill. I remember getting it in Yankee Stadium, the sixth one off Al Downing on a Friday night. On Saturday Whitey Ford pitched, and I hit a ball up the middle, and I thought it was going to be a base hit. But [Tony] Kubek threw me out by half a step. But it was nice to get the sixth one and at least be in the record books until 1981.

"Actually, I had the fifth one in Detroit on a Thursday, and we went into Yankee Stadium on a Friday. I sat there, and Al Downing is pitching. I'm thinking to myself, 'What should I look for? I want to try to get the best advantage I can.' And so I'm figuring he's going to maybe start me out with a breaking ball, because there are men on base, and I'm pinch hitting, and we still have a chance to win the ball game. I'm looking for a breaking ball, and he throws me one right down the middle for strike one. And I thought, 'Man, I hope I didn't blow it here.' Then there were a couple of balls, and then I fouled one off. Then he threw a breaking ball, a high slider, and I got a double to left field. I was glad to get that one.

"Another big thrill was up on the Yankee-Fan-O-Gram. It indicated that was an American League record, that particular pinch hit that I just got. So that was kind of exciting."

Johnson, who came from Nebraska, was a small player at 5-foot-10, 175 pounds, yet he picked up a nickname that's usually associated with big sluggers—"Rocky."

"Bill Tuttle gave me the nickname Rocky in 1960 when I was playing with Kansas City. Bill Tuttle was our center fielder, and he started calling me Little Rocky Colavito. It kind of stuck with me. Now even on my business card I have Rocky Johnson."

Once Johnson even got mistaken for his namesake, Rocky Colavito.

"Brooks [Robinson] and I roomed together for four years and one month. After a night game in Cleveland one time, we went up to the Sheraton Cleveland, where we were staying. We

Bob Johnson. *Baltimore Orioles Photos*

went in the Kon Tiki Room there, where we were going to have dinner. While we were eating, we were up on a kind of upper level, I noticed that these guys kind of kept looking over at us, a couple guys. I figured they're probably coming over for an autograph. Well, sure enough, one guy comes over, and he's got a few programs with him. He comes over, and he stands right in front of the table, and he says to me, 'You're Rocky Colavito, aren't you?' And I said, 'Yes, I am.' He said, 'My kids would sure love to have your autograph. And some of the other guys would, too. Would you mind signing this?' And I'm saying, 'I'd be glad to.' He also said, 'You know, you look smaller out of uniform.' So I said, 'Yeah, that uniform makes you look a little bigger, you know.' And I say to Brooks, 'How do you spell Colavito?'

"So I'm signing it, and I finish, and he says, 'I really appreciate that.' And then he says, looking at Brooks Robinson, 'By the way, is this one of the ball players here?' So I say, 'He's this new guy, he just came up from the minor leagues.' So the guy reaches over and shakes Brooks' hand and says, 'Congratulations, I hope you have a great career.' Had he known he was Brooks Robinson, he would have had a Hall of Famer on his scorecard. We laughed about it, but I hope the guy never found that out."

CHAPTER 15

Center of Attention:
Paul Blair
(1964-1976)

An eight-time Gold Glove recipient, Paul Blair was the best center fielder in Orioles history. He was a bulwark of the team's first four World Series teams and even supplied a pesky bat from time to time.

Blair patrolled the outfield in a way that appeared effortless but in fact required exquisite skill and artistry. He loved playing shallow, almost daring hitters to make him run back to the wall to snatch an extra-base hit away from them. At least once, however, that approach did not sit well with his manager.

"We were in Minnesota playing the first game of a doubleheader. In the bottom of the ninth inning, bases loaded, Jim Holt hits the ball to the top of the wall in left-center field. He's a left-handed hitter. And we lose the ball game.

"I come off the field, and Earl says, 'If you weren't playing so close, so shallow, you'd have caught that ball.' I said, 'Earl, it hit off the top of the fence, 15 feet high. I know I can sky a little bit, but I couldn't have caught that ball.' He said, '*You* would have caught it.'

"So the second game of the doubleheader, we go out and score five runs in the first inning. I go out to center field in the old Minnesota ballpark, where it's 430 to center field. I was standing in the middle of the warning track, 425 feet away. And I stayed out there the whole game. Fortunately, we won, 11-1. But in the bottom of the eighth, the Minnesota shortstop hits a ground ball up the middle for a single, and it wound up being a double because I was so deep I couldn't get to it. So after that game, Earl says, 'Are you going to play right?' I said, 'Earl, you told me not to let the ball get over my head.' He said, 'Well, I can't tell you nothin' anyway. Do what you want.' And he left me alone from then on."

Blair joined the Orioles before Weaver did, coming to the majors for good in 1965 under manager Hank Bauer. He had wowed Bauer with his defensive prowess, and the manager, despite some misgivings from the front office, wanted to keep the fielding whiz on the big-league roster.

"I'd missed 12 days of spring training because I was in the army reserves. Fortunately for me, I had a real good spring and made the ball club. Opening Day was so exciting for me, because you're fulfilling a lifelong dream. I was in center field on that Opening Day in 1965. We won the game, and I'm a bona fide major leaguer."

Though he always will be remembered for his outfield play, Blair occasionally had some pop in his bat. In 1969 he slugged 26 home runs and hit 124 regular-season homers in his 13 years as an Oriole. The biggest hit of his career came in the third game of the 1966 World Series. It was the first World Series game ever to be played in Baltimore. The Orioles had won the first two games against the Dodgers in Los Angeles.

"It was in the fifth inning, and Claude Osteen threw me a fastball, and I hit it out of the park, and we win the game, 1-0. I was kind of looking for the fastball, and he threw me one on the inside part of the plate. And as soon as I hit it, I knew it was gone.

"Everyone said I should have taken my time and gotten to trot around the bases, but I never trotted. I just liked to hit my

Paul Blair. *Baltimore Orioles Photos*

home runs and get back to the dugout. Because back in those days, you hit a home run and the next time you came up, they wanted to knock you down. So I never wanted to try and show up the pitcher. We only had three hits that whole game, and one of them was my bases-empty home run.

"The next day Frank [Robinson] hits the home run to give us a 1-0 lead. I came in in the eighth inning. Jim LeFebvre hits a ball to straight-away center field, and I go back and jump up and I catch it. So I saved that home run, and we wind up winning again, 1-0.

"It's my second full year in the big leagues, and I'm on a world championship team. We played the Los Angeles Dodgers, and I'm from Los Angeles. They didn't want to sign me, so that was real good payback to be on the winning team that beat the Dodgers in '66."

Blair felt proud of both his winning home run in the third game and his catch that preserved the victory in the Series-clinching fourth game. But for the fielding wizard, the home run had special meaning.

"To hit a home run in the World Series, and you win, 1-0, and four years ago you're in high school, that's an all-time great feeling. The home run was a wonderful, wonderful feeling, because through all of my boyhood, you see World Series, and you sit there and fantasize, and here it comes true. A lifetime vision comes true. I hit a home run and we win, 1-0. The catch was fine, too, but catching—that was my forte. I was always pretty good with the glove and wound up being a pretty good center fielder."

Another momentous time for Blair—and for the Orioles—came a month earlier in Kansas City, when the club clinched its first American League pennant, beating the then-KC Athletics, 6-1. The Orioles had a rousing celebration that continued from Kansas City, on the plane ride to Los Angeles and at the hotel after they arrived in Anaheim. Many of the players were not in the best condition to play that next evening against the Angels.

"It was something that I'd never been involved in. I'd never drink, but I drank some champagne that night. That was basically all we were doing—hoopin' and hollerin' and drinkin' champagne.

The thing I remember most, I got to my room, and I was just so sick. I said, 'I don't understand how they drink like this,' because, man, I was sick, and I think I threw up. That was the last time I drank champagne. From then on, when we won or clinched anything, I just took the champagne and spread it on everybody. I didn't want to drink it anymore. I still don't drink. That was the first time I drank, and it basically was the last."

In the beginning of 1965 and part of 1966, Blair platooned in center field with Russ Snyder, a good-hitting left-handed batter. But eventually, Blair gained most of the playing time during the regular season. "It was a little frustrating sharing center field, but it was really my first and second years in the big leagues, and, hey, you're just glad to be there. You've got to earn your spot. He'd been there, so I had to earn my spot and take that position. And eventually I did. But I really had no problem with [platooning] at the time, because I wanted to be in the big leagues. I didn't like sitting on the bench, that's for sure. So my whole theory was, if I'm head and shoulders the best outfielder on my team, I'm going to get to play through my slumps. That's what I wanted to do. And if I could save my pitchers some runs, they're going to almost demand that I play center field. Back then, our main principle was, if we didn't allow too many runs, we don't have to score too many runs. Our whole thing was pitching and defense. And I could cover more ground than anybody out there, and I think I saved the pitchers quite a few runs. So consequently I got to play every day. And that's what I wanted to do."

CHAPTER 16

Earl's Best Bud:
Jim Palmer
(1965-1984)

J im Palmer clearly is the best pitcher in Orioles history. The right-hander was voted into the baseball Hall of Fame in 1990 on the first ballot for which he was eligible.

He has more wins than any pitcher in club history and is at or near the top in almost every statistical category for Baltimore starting pitchers. He recorded 53 shutouts and an astonishing—by today's standards—211 complete games during his career. Eight times he won 20 or more games, and three times Palmer, now an Orioles broadcaster, was named American League Cy Young Award winner.

He was meticulous in his approach to pitching, and his intelligence helped him on the mound almost as much as his right arm. On August 13, 1969, Palmer pitched a no-hitter against Oakland, beating the A's, 8-0.

"At that point I'd come back, I'd had my back problems in '69, so I'd missed like 50-some days, 52 days, 53 days, at about $1,000 a game. I'd had a bonus because I'd been hurt the two previous years, for $500 for winning anywhere between 10 and 14 and anything over 14 wins, I got $1,000 per game. I'd come back from

Jim Palmer. *Baltimore Orioles Photos*

the back problems, and I pitched six innings against the Twins, giving up one run. And then the start against Oakland. It was the perfect game to pitch a no-hitter, other than that they had a pretty good hitting team. It was Oakland with [Bert] Campaneris and those kind of guys. The interesting thing is that Belanger didn't play that night, Bobby Floyd played short, and Don Buford, who was usually our left fielder, was playing second base. The only guys I had [from the regular infield] were Boog and Brooks—which is not too bad. But I got eight runs, and of course I knew I had a no-hitter going. If you don't know you've got a no-hitter, you're not a very aware pitcher. And I like to think that even in 1969, I was. So I knew I had a no-hitter. [After walking Reggie Jackson and getting Sal Bando to fly out to center to start the ninth] I got Danny Cater to hit a bouncing ball for a double play, and Bobby Floyd dropped it, but got the force at second. Dick Green came up, and I went 0-2, and I threw him three perfect pitches, they maybe missed by about half an inch, and the umpire didn't call any of them. Then I walked him. Then they sent up Tommy Reynolds, and I didn't know who Tommy Reynolds was. He was an outfielder. And I looked on deck, and there was Larry Haney, and I knew Larry, because he had played in our organization. In fact, he had caught me in the instructional league. So I figured with Reynolds, I'm here to make my pitches, and I got behind him, and I walked him. And at 8-0 [the score of the game], you're not going to worry about losing the game with two outs in the ninth. So the bases were loaded. Larry Haney came up, and he was a pull hitter, and I threw him a fastball away, and he hit a ground ball to shortstop.

"It's interesting, I now see Larry Haney because he's an advance scout with Milwaukee. And he always says, 'My mom and my wife were big fans of yours, and they were actually hoping that I made an out.' So I say, 'Well, good, I'm glad. I'm glad to hear that.'"

After the game, though, Palmer says he felt no special sense of elation, as one might expect from a pitcher who's just hurled a no-hitter. He was just happy to be back on the mound again after his injury.

"No, when you come back from an arm injury and back injuries like I had, you're just happy to be out there. And actually, I tried to score on a short fly ball to Reggie Jackson in right field, and [catcher] Dave Duncan kind of put his foot out, and I got flipped and landed on my heel. So it was just another journey, another chapter in the journey of coming back and proving I could still pitch in the big leagues. I came back and pitched very well. I was 10-2 when I'd hurt my back. I'd just kind of had one leg shorter than the other. I eventually found Russell Wright, who was the team physician in Detroit, and he was also the team doctor for the U.S. Olympic weight lifting team. So he was really into back injuries, and he found out what was wrong…and put a lift in, and I never really had any back problems again."

Another one of Palmer's distinctions is that he's the only pitcher in baseball history to win World Series games in three different decades—the 1960s, '70s, and '80s. He pitched a shutout to win the second game of the 1966 Series, the Orioles' first appearance in postseason play. It was the first of three shutouts the team threw to sweep the Dodgers in 1966. And what made his 6-0 win in the second game even more memorable was that it was against Sandy Koufax, in what would be the Dodger star lefty's final performance in a major league game. Palmer was 20 at the time and was the youngest pitcher at that point ever to hurl a shutout in a World Series game.

The Orioles had won the first game of the Series, 5-2, scoring three runs in the first inning—more than the Dodgers would score the entire series. They held on to win that game thanks to the relief work of Moe Drabowsky. That opening game win helped Palmer build up his confidence for his outing in Los Angeles the next afternoon.

"I think that first whole World Series game, when Brooks and Frank hit home runs in the first inning, guys said, 'Gee, maybe we have a chance to win here.' Of course, Don Drysdale was tough, but they might not have done that against Koufax. That was because of Jewish holidays and having him pitch the last Sunday of the season. What set up that whole World Series, we had a nice scouting report and all that, but then we had Moe

Drabowsky come in. I always wondered if Dave McNally hadn't been knocked out early [in Game 1], hadn't struggled early, and Moe hadn't come in and struck out 11 Dodgers in six and two-thirds innings, would I have had the confidence that I had when I went out there. It's not that I was as good as Moe Drabowsky, because I wasn't. I won 15 games, but Moe could hit his spots, he had a terrific breaking ball, and an overpowering fastball. He was a great guy to have in the bullpen, and he just came in and just overpowered the Dodgers with high fastballs. So I kind of got the message, sitting there. But I think when you're 20 years old pitching against Koufax, you're just kind of thinking about not embarrassing yourself and getting through your first World Series game. I guess the irony is that it was my first shutout ever at the major-league level. I picked a pretty good time to do it, I suppose."

Palmer is the only Oriole to be on all six of the club's World Series teams. He picked up his final postseason win in relief over the Phillies in the third game of the 1983 Series, which the Orioles went on to win, four games to one.

"In that last World Series, I was hurt that year and had to go to [minor-league affiliate] Hagerstown. I hurt my back early and tried to pitch through it. I threw 139 pitches, like my first game back, and thought I tore my rotator cuff. It was a torturous summer for me, but the club was playing well. While I was not a great part of that, at least I was able to be on the roster in the playoffs and the World Series. I was sitting out in the bullpen in Philadelphia thinking, 'You know, there are a lot of people paying a lot more to watch this game that are a lot further away from home plate than me. And I'm going to get a World Series check.' As it turned out, I lucked out. I came in and got through two innings, even though I really hadn't been pitching a whole lot in relief. And a ball goes through Ivan DeJesus' legs, and all of a sudden I became the only guy to ever win a World Series game in three different decades. It wasn't quite as dramatic as the first win in the 1966 World Series, but it was on my birthday, and it was a nice 37th birthday present."

Palmer had many remarkable achievements as a pitcher, including his Cy Young awards and 20-win seasons. But one of the most interesting achievements was that in more than 4,000 innings—including his World Series and playoff appearances—he never yielded a grand slam. He credits both luck and his own determination not to give up a home run when he faced a batter with the bases full.

"Who would ever want to give up four runs in one swing? I was pretty good at math, so I learned early on, one's better than four. But I think there's certainly a luck factor in it. Back in 1980, 1981 or 1982, somewhere in that range, Weaver wanted me to walk John Lowenstein to get to Al Oliver and load the bases up to set up a double play. And I looked at him, and I go, 'That's a horrible idea.' He said, 'Yeah, you might throw a double-play ball.' I said, 'I'm a fly ball pitcher, when was the last time I threw a ground ball for a double play?' And I said, 'Do you really want me to do this?' And he said, 'Yeah.' So I said, 'I'll tell you what. I'll go manage, and you pitch. Because this is a horrible idea.' And he said, 'Walk him,' and he ran off the mound. So I walked Lowenstein, and I told Rick Dempsey, 'Just set low and away.' Because Bill Stein was on deck, and he didn't hit home runs. So I figured, I'll walk in a run before giving up a grand slam. I was at like 3,500 innings. I'm almost at the end of my career. Why would I want to be throwing—first of all, why would I even want to walk John Lowenstein to get to Al Oliver? We were already down. DeCinces had come in on a ball and thrown it away. They were ahead, 3-0, and we hadn't scored four runs in a month. So I knew we'd already lost. It was just kind of a forgone conclusion. So we walk Lowenstein, and Dempsey forgets that I said low and away. He puts down a fastball, and I start my wind-up, and he moves up and in. I had really just started my hands, well I just stepped off the mound. If you're thinking low and away, and the catcher's setting up and in, the ball's probably going to go right down the middle. I figured I'd been through too many battles, too many innings, to throw a grand slam in this situation. Joe Brinkman was the umpire at second base, and I hear him call, 'Balk.' I was never so happy in my life. I balked in a run, but now the bases weren't loaded.

"In 1978 I was going for win number 19 and I had the bases loaded and nobody out going against Dennis Eckersley. It was 1-1. I had Bruce Bochy, and he struck out; Andy Thornton popped up; and Rico Carty took the first two pitches to go 2-0. And I go, 'Okay, I better take a little bit off and just throw him a strike away.' He hits this fly ball to left field, and Bumbry goes back and back and back. It wasn't hit very hard, but the wind was blowing out—the fences were in that year—and he catches it as it's going over the wall. That was the closest I ever came to throwing a grand slam, period."

The verbal and mental contretemps between Palmer and Weaver were legendary. Every player who wore the Orioles uniform during the days when the Hall of Fame pitcher and the Hall of Fame manager were together can tell stories of their battles. Each one always wanted to get in the last word. In many ways, they were opposites. Weaver was tiny, a bantam rooster. Palmer was tall and lanky. Weaver was feisty and coarse, Palmer smooth and sophisticated. Both had tremendous pride, though, and each thought he knew what was best, that he was always right and the other always wrong. Their sparring sessions on the mound are a classic chapter in Orioles folklore.

"There was a Sunday afternoon game, I forget the year, but it must have been sometime in the early '70s. I walked a couple of guys; Belanger made two errors. We're talking about a guy who won eight or nine Gold Gloves. Boog dropped a ball in foul territory that he lost in the sun. All this in the first inning. I gave up two runs, and in the middle of this two-run rally for the Twins, Weaver came running out, and he says, 'Are you trying?'—with a profanity in there. And I go, 'Am I trying?' I said, 'You made out the lineup. You put Belanger at shortstop. Do you think he was trying to make two errors? Or better yet,' I said, 'Why don't you go ask Boog over there'—at about 290 pounds—'whether he tried to drop that ball in foul territory.' I said, 'If you don't really have anything intelligent to say to me, and worthwhile and constructive, why don't you get out of here?' And I threw a few profanities in. And he said, 'Okay.' And then he ran off the mound. Are you trying! That was just that one. We had all kinds. There are so many.

"Actually, one of the funniest is, I had a 102-degree temperature, and I was pitching against Texas. I really wasn't feeling well. I get them out in the first inning at Memorial Stadium, and we get five runs in the bottom of the inning. I come in, and it's Weaver and [pitching coach George] Bamberger and then me. I'm sitting there and Weaver looks over, and he leans across George, and he says, 'Just think how bad you'd feel if you'd stayed home tonight.' Because it was now 5-0, and I was on my way to a win. And I looked at him, and I go, 'That's one of the smartest things you've ever said, Earl.' And he was right on."

Few players actually liked Weaver, but almost all give him credit for knowing how to manage. Palmer is no exception, although he admits his personal relationship with the colorful Orioles skipper was particularly antagonistic.

"It was contentious, because he wanted me to be perfect, and I couldn't do it. I'd sit there for three days and go out there and pitch the fourth day, and I knew how he was in the dugout. We always talk about the negative-positive. Well, he'd always give you all the negatives. 'Don't walk this guy.' 'Can't get beat. You have a one-run lead.' It would be about the ninth inning, and you'd be thinking, 'Okay, I'm going to be aggressive, I'm going to go out there, and I'm not going to walk anybody.' And as your feet would hit the cinder track, he'd go, 'Can't get beat until you walk somebody.' That was just negative-positive. He'd give you all the negatives. Like Richie Dauer used to hit into a lot of double plays, and Weaver finally said, 'Just pop up once in a while.' His idea was, that would only be one out. Another negative. That was Earl. Weaver-isms.

"On a club with a lot of continuity, which we had, it really didn't matter. There was so much continuity between the older players and the younger players, and the old players and the newly arrived players, that it didn't matter. Earl knew how to manage, and we knew how to deal with him. For us, he really gave me a lot of responsibility to win or lose games. And for that, I pitched a lot of complete games and got a lot of wins. And I probably got some losses I might not have gotten. But every year that he managed us, we had a chance to win the pennant. I don't know of too many people who can go through a whole career, where every year I went to spring training, we had a chance to win. That's pretty special. And Earl was part of that. Could somebody else maybe manage as well? I don't know. All I know is that he did, and he handled a lot of different players, from Reggie Jackson to Frank Robinson to Earl Williams to whatever, and we kept winning. And that's really what this game is all about."

CHAPTER 17

The Prankster:
Moe Drabowsky
(1966-1968; 1970)

The Orioles have had many pranksters on their rosters over the years, but none were more adept at the art of mischief than pitcher Moe Drabowsky. He knew how to exploit the vulnerabilities of his teammates, and whenever the chance arose, he jumped in to play a trick on someone. Even the commissioner of baseball was fair prey under Drabowsky's rules of roguishness. He pitched out of the bullpen for the world championship team in 1966. And even though he set a record for strikeouts by a reliever and got the victory in the first game of that Series, his pranks were so pernicious that some of his teammates probably wished he had never set foot in the Orioles' clubhouse, especially those who had to deal with Drabowsky's snakes.

"It really started with Frank Robinson. Frank would carry an attaché case. Back then every player didn't carry attaché cases. We didn't have agents, so we had no reason to walk around and bring any files with us. We didn't have laptops back then, no cell phones. We were just in our own little world, 25 guys together. Frank was the only one with an attaché case. We kidded him about it day in and day out. One day on the bus we were agitating Frank and saying, 'Hey, what've you got in there, what's in that attaché case?' So he opened it up, and he reached in and grabbed something and threw it toward the back of the bus. And what he had was a huge rubber snake inside the attaché. And the players were petrified. So I thought, 'Hey I've got to substitute a live snake for the rubber one, and we'll see some more great activity.'

"Frank had a combination lock, so you couldn't get into his attaché case. So what happened was, when we got out to California, I went to a pet shop and picked up a boa constrictor and some garter snakes and even some white mice. I went to the ballpark and had all of these things in a bag. But when I got to the park, all the white mice were gone, and I said, 'What in the world happened to the mice?' And then I looked at some of the snakes, and they had this huge bulge in their bodies. The guy at the pet shop had guaranteed me that the snakes had been fed and wouldn't eat the mice, but he lied. So at the ballpark I had the boa constrictor wrapped around my head, and [Paul] Blair came in, and he thought it was a rubber snake. So he really wasn't too petrified. But then he saw its tongue flick out a number of times, and he was in reverse very quickly and out in the dugout, and out on the field. He wouldn't come back in the clubhouse. He was petrified of me and didn't want to be around me at all after that. And with Luis Aparicio, I would put a couple of smaller snakes in his uniform pants pockets, and hang his pants back up in his locker. Of course, I'd have to be there early before the bus arrived. And with Charlie Lau, I'd put the boa constrictor on a hanger. The snakes would like to wrap around things like a hanger. Then I'd put his uniform shirt back on the hanger and button it up. Then I'd go over in the corner and sit and watch these guys as they came in and started to get dressed. So Luis would be dressing and put his pants on, he's getting ready to buckle his belt, and I could see this pained expression on his face. And then he'd realize that there was something crawling on him—something was irritating his butt—that something was moving in his pants pocket. You could not believe how quickly he zipped those pants down, was out of them in no time at all, and flew out of the clubhouse. And poor Charlie Lau, he's getting ready to put his shirt on, and he

Moe Drabowsky. *Baltimore Orioles Photos*

went over and unbuttoned it, and there's that snake head with its tongue flicking out. Charlie was absolutely petrified, too. We got Charlie and Luis and Camilo Carreon all pretty much in one day. Camilo was writing names down on the pass list, and I dropped a snake between his right elbow and his rib right onto the pass list. And Camilo just tore out of the clubhouse, also. I was pretty bad, when I look back at it."

Bad, perhaps, but undaunted. Perhaps even more mischievous than his snake act were Drabowsky's shenanigans with the bullpen phone in Kansas City.

"I had played with the Kansas City Athletics for three years and came over to Baltimore, having been the player rep in Kansas City. They had a direct dial system throughout the ballpark, and I knew all the phone numbers at the different locations. They were all three-digit numbers. The press box had a certain number, the radio booth, the owner's box, the clubhouse, the dugout, the bullpen, things of that nature. It was a Friday night. I hadn't had a chance to check my buddies on the Kansas City ball club, so we're getting shut out, 2-0, by Jim Nash, a big right-hander for Kansas City. About the sixth inning, I called over to the Kansas City bullpen. I was going to talk to a couple of players to bring me up to date about what was going on in Kansas City. And when a coach answered the phone, I just yelled in the phone quickly, 'Get Krausse hot in a hurry!' Then I hung up the phone. So the coach thought it was the manager calling, and all of a sudden Lew Krausse, a right-handed pitcher, came out of the bullpen dugout, along with a catcher. They got out very quickly and started to warm up very feverishly, and we just doubled up with laughter on our side. We laughed the rest of the game. After about two or three minutes, I called back and said, 'Well, that's enough. Sit him down!' So down they went.

"Stories get exaggerated sometimes with the passage of time. And one writer mentioned that Drabowsky deserves one more victory in his won-loss record because Nash got very upset as he looked down to the bullpen and saw a relief pitcher warming up when he was working on a two-hit shutout. So he lost his concentration and composure, and we came back to beat them.

Unfortunately, that's not true. He did shut us out. And as we came into the clubhouse after the game, we were still very much in a jovial mood. We just couldn't believe you could manipulate an opposing team's bullpen with a simple call. The writers wanted to know why we were cracking up. So we told them the story. So it made the AP and UPI, and my fan mail increased very dramatically shortly thereafter. I got one little letter from some kid in Keokuk, Iowa, that said, 'Baseball needs more nuts like you.' I never did it again, but I was thinking of doing it sometime after I got out of baseball. I could call from anywhere in the country. I was tempted to do it, but I thought [it best] to leave it alone."

After the Orioles' World Series victory over Cincinnati in 1970, however, Drabowsky never considered leaving the commissioner of baseball alone.

"I gave Commissioner Bowie Kuhn a severe hot foot in 1970, after we beat the Cincinnati Reds in the World Series. He came into the clubhouse, and I put a whole book of matches, 20 matches, pretty close to the heel of his shoe. Then I ran a trail of lighter fluid from the matches back to a point where I couldn't be seen. Then I lit the lighter fluid and you could see this trail of flame going from where I was, heading toward the commissioner and toward the matches as he was having a conversation with a couple of people. It hit the matches, and it was like a miniature bomb going off—an explosion and flames. We got him pretty good."

The Orioles had a beloved trainer, Ralph Salvon, during the Drabowsky years. He was a very close friend of many players, and he also became the butt of one of Drabowsky's conniving schemes.

"I got Ralph Salvon, our trainer, very, very good one night. He would give me rubdowns, and sometimes he could hurt you a little bit. I told him, 'Hey, I'm going to get even with you one of these nights, because you were stretching me a little too much the other night. I'll get you.' So we were on the road somewhere, and I called the hotel front desk, and I told the gal, 'This is Ralph Salvon. I'm the trainer of the Orioles. I'm not in my room right now, but I want to leave a wake-up call. I want a wake-up call at

1, 3, 5, 7, and 9.' The gal said, 'What was that? A wake-up call for what?' And I said, 'For 1, 3, 5, 7, and 9.' She said, 'That's kind of unusual.' I said, 'I want a wake-up call for 1 a.m., 3 a.m., 5 a.m., 7 a.m., and 9 a.m.' I said, 'I've got this severe eye infection. I must take these eye drops every two hours or I will go blind. So if I don't answer the phone, you can have somebody come up and knock on the door. And if I do answer the phone, I'll be groggy and I'll tell you if there are any other calls for the night, cancel them. Do not, under any circumstances, cancel any calls. Just keep coming back to me.' So I had him pretty good. He got calls every two hours all night long. Ralph did not look too good the next day."

Drabowsky was not all play and no work, however. His pitching performance in the first World Series game in Orioles history propelled the team to sweep the Dodgers that year. He entered the game to replace starter Dave McNally in the third inning and made a thin lead hold up the rest of the game, not allowing a single Dodger to score.

"It was a fantastic thrill. When the Series began, my only goal was that I hoped to get in the Series, because I wanted to see my name in a World Series box score somewhere down the road, many years from now. That was all I had in mind. To experience what happened was certainly never in my game plan. It's not something I desired. As I said, I'd have been happy to pitch to one hitter. But to go ahead and pitch 6 2/3 innings and win the ball game and kind of set the tone for the rest of the games was an unbelievable feeling. There's nothing like championship baseball. The players make so much money nowadays that they have everything that they want—except they don't have the championship ring. You see a lot of these guys who have played, and they want the championship ring. That motivates a lot of guys. That's a goal they have. So it was beyond my wildest dreams to experience what happened in 1966, and to strike out a lot of guys [11 in 6 2/3 innings]. I tied one record, most strikeouts in a row—six—and my 11 strikeouts were the most ever by a relief pitcher. That'll be pretty difficult to break, because the situation doesn't happen much in today's game—where a relief pitcher comes in in the third inning and then pitches the rest of the game."

(editors note: Drabowsky, who served the Orioles as a minor league pitching coach, died on June 10, 2006.)

CHAPTER 18

A Game of Firsts:
Eddie Watt
(1966-1973)

Eddie Watt was a standout Orioles reliever during the team's early glory years. A member of the club's first four World Series teams, Watt was from Iowa, and he never had been to a big-league stadium until the first day of the 1966 championship season for the Orioles. As it turned out, Watt got to pitch in the first big-league game he ever attended.

"Growing up very poor in Iowa, I had never had the opportunity to witness a big-league game in person. We never made it to Chicago or St. Louis or anywhere else. The first major-league baseball game I saw was Opening Day in 1966, and I pitched the bottom of the 13th inning. It was the first big-league game I had witnessed in person. I had seen some minor-league games in Cedar Rapids, but never a big-league game.

"I had made the club in spring training. And I got a save in the game on Opening Day because we got the winning run in the top of the 13th. Pitching that first time in the big leagues was a feeling you can't describe, and if you try, you never can do it accurately or well. It was the culmination of a childhood dream,

Eddie Watt. *Baltimore Orioles Photos*

and something I had wanted all my life. I had just turned 25. I was very nervous and very excited, all that adrenaline was going.

"It was a one-two-three inning. George Scott was the first hitter I faced. I had faced him the year before in the minor leagues. I struck Scott out. Then Rico Petrocelli hit a ground out to Brooks at third. The third hitter was Tony Horton, and Tony hit a little grounder back to me. It was a thrill. Joining the big league club like that was a little easier than it would have been in certain cases, because we had eight first-year players—guys like [Paul] Blair, Davey Johnson, [Andy] Etchebarren, Gene Brabender. We had a bunch of young guys, and all except Brabender had come up through the system. And Boog [Powell] and Dave McNally were younger than I was, and they were already on the team. The only real established stars were Frank and Brooks Robinson. And Steve Barber was there, but he got hurt and only pitched half the year. Frank was about 30, and he was probably the oldest, except for maybe Russ Snyder, who was probably in his 30s.

"The biggest thing I remember about the Orioles from then is the players, not so much the games or a particular game or incident. Life was different then than it is now. Now players go from one team to the next. Our ball club stayed together then. We would go year after year and make maybe one or two or three changes. But the nucleus stayed pretty much intact for the seven or eight years I was with the Orioles. There was day-to-day association among the players.

"Of course we did a lot of wild and silly things. But the most important thing was the day-to-day interactions, the friendships, knowing and being able to rely on each other for everything and anything that came up. I think that was the most outstanding thing about the Orioles back then. It was just a feeling. I always felt if I truly needed something, there was any number of people I could ask for help. And I would give help to anyone myself—the managers and coaches as well as the players.

"I got there the first year that Jerry Hoffberger bought the club. He was an outstanding person. You felt very much at home talking to him. Even though he was wealthy and powerful, he always made you feel as an equal. It was the whole line like that in the organization, from top to bottom.

Watt joined the Orioles before Earl Weaver became the team's manager in 1968. But the unassuming reliever had already played for Weaver back at Double-A Elmira before he was promoted to Baltimore in 1966. Watt performed a rare feat at Elmira: He pitched two no-hitters, and in between those two gems, he threw a shutout.

"It was in Elmira, in 1965, and Earl was our manager. The first no-hitter was on Opening Day in Elmira. Then we went on the road, and I pitched in a 0-0 game, and we came back to Elmira and I pitched another no-hitter.

"Earl was a very good manager. Earl is older than I am, but not noticeably. He had a very good baseball mind then. In any ballgame that he was connected with, you never had to worry about being out-managed. Earl was way ahead of the game, inning by inning. He knew what was going on well in advance. He had tremendous foresight. He was demanding, but the only thing he demanded was that you gave your full effort and enjoyed yourself out on the field. Earl had a tremendous knack of never asking you to do something you couldn't do.

"I don't think anybody enjoyed playing for the Orioles more than I did. Sometimes I wish I could have played a little longer."

CHAPTER 19

The Steaming Teapot:
Earl Weaver
(1968-1982; 1985-1986)

Earl Weaver always gave off the impression of being a man who knew no fear. The Orioles Hall of Fame manager was blustery and oozed self-confidence—at least in appearance. But when he was named manager in the midst of the 1968 season, after having begun the year as the club's first base coach, he admits to being scared.

"What was it like when I first was named manager? It was scary. After spending 20 years in the minor leagues, nine as a player and 11 as a minor-league manager, I finally was rewarded after getting a coaching job in Baltimore and starting to get time on the pension, which was the big thing for me. The Orioles had won in '66. The reason they dropped off in '67 was that Frank Robinson had slid into [a collision at] second base and got double vision. And when you lose a player like Frank, it hurts. I felt pretty secure that the Orioles were going to win again when Frank got healthy.

"It was a good organization, and I knew a lot of the young ball players that were coming up. We had a good minor-league system at the time, and I was very familiar with it. So I thought,

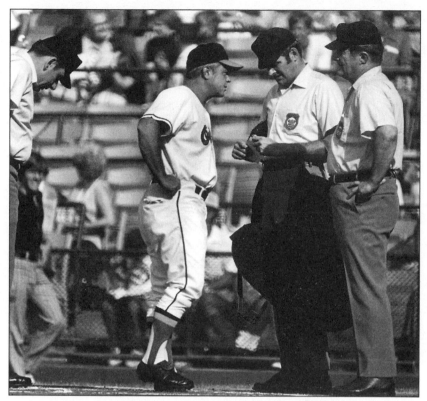

Earl Weaver. *Baltimore Orioles Photos*

'Okay, first base coaching job, do your thing, hit your fungoes, do the job at first base, help the organization in any way you can, just like I did in the minor leagues.' And as a result, when things weren't going right—again Frank got the mumps early in the year, and he still was having some double vision in the first half of the [1968] season—all of a sudden we found ourselves 13 or 14 games out of first place.

"That's when Harry Dalton, the general manager, decided to make the change and name me as manager. And it was scary, because I had spent 20 years in the minor leagues, working my way up. I was rewarded with the coaching job in the major leagues, which was pretty simple—no decisions to make or anything else.

Just do what you're told and do your job. And all of a sudden, here you are, managing a ball club, and you know that if you don't win—and it was an interim [job] anyway—you're going to be back in the minor leagues, or without a job altogether.

"I thought that eventually, if you run out of teams to manage in the minor leagues, that you're going to go to scouting. And my baseball judgment was pretty good as far as recommending players to the organization when I was in the minor leagues, and for drafting players. I was pretty proud of my baseball judgment. From the number of guys you could look at and say, 'Okay, this guy's going to the major leagues, and we might as well release this guy right now.' At any rate, two and a half years is about the average life of a major league manager with any one club. So I'm thinking, 'How the heck am I ever going to get my five years in on the pension?' You needed five years to qualify at that time. Well, it was scary. And my wife, when I was named manager, she said, 'Is that good?' And I said, 'I don't know. I'll tell you maybe two or three or four years from now.' So, it all worked out well."

The frightening part for Weaver was simply the insecurity of holding onto a managing job in the big leagues. As far as running the club and handling the decision-making responsibilities, he had no worries.

"It's the same as in the minor leagues. There was no problem with managing the ball club. It was just, how good is the ball club going to be? Or how good am I going to be? I told my wife after the '68 season that I was the best manager in the major leagues at the time. That might have been true, or it might not have been, because there were a lot of good managers up there. But I had a great ball club. And I knew I could handle that ball club the way it should be handled."

Weaver could resemble a steaming teapot when he walked onto the diamond to argue an umpire's call or dress down a player in the dugout. By the next day, however, he always seemed to have simmered down. He credits the talent of his ballplayers for making the job easy for him and enabling him to check his temper almost as soon as it had boiled over.

"I'd take it home, but I'd never cut off my nose to spite my face. When you've got great guys, though, it becomes so easy. It was just about impossible to do anything wrong with that ball club in '68, '69, and '70. We were a group—there was no free agency at the time—who knew we were going to stick together. The biggest problem was the guys trying to get a raise for next year. Back then, you either played for what they offered you, or you didn't play. I don't know if that was right, but it kept the club together, and we had a great ball club."

Never, perhaps, in the history of the Baltimore Orioles, did its fans offer a more spontaneous and heart-felt appreciation to a member of the team than they did on the final day of the 1982 season. It was Weaver's 15th consecutive year in the Orioles dugout, and the manager already had announced that he planned to retire following the season. The Orioles began the campaign very slowly, and it wasn't until June 8 that they pulled themselves above the .500 mark. They still were not in the pennant chase, though, until they went 17-1, beginning on August 20. They kept pecking away and with four days left in the season, they trailed the first-place Milwaukee Brewers by three games—with the Brewers coming to Memorial Stadium for those final four games.

The Orioles miraculously won the first three games, pulling into a tie with Milwaukee and turning the final game into Russian roulette. The conqueror would go to the postseason; the vanquished would go home the next day. Milwaukee easily won the final game, dashing the hopes of Orioles fans, but not their love and enthusiasm for their team and their departing manager. As the Brewers were celebrating their victory, Orioles fans remained at the stadium, cheering for Weaver and his players. Some 45 minutes after the season officially had ended in disappointment, Weaver returned to the field and led the still-cheering fans in a rousing O-R-I-O-L-E-S chant that shook the old ballpark to its foundations. But Weaver was resolute about his decision to retire.

"After 15 years, there's burnout. I was tired of arguing with the umpires, believe it or not. I didn't enjoy that. I was ashamed of myself when I went home, every time I got thrown out of a game. And naturally, when you have to do things like tell Brooks Robinson that you're going to bench him, and put in Doug DeCinces at third base—not that there's anything wrong with that—time marches on, and when I had to get on the phone after the '71 season, and run down Frank Robinson and tell him that we traded him, those things hurt. Releasing a guy like Lee May, one of the nicest people that you've ever known, by saying, 'Look, we have no place for you to play,' let alone hollering at guys, trying to get them in line…all those are heartbreaking things.

"Don Buford is another one. He did everything I ever asked of him. But Don Baylor was coming out of the minor leagues —that's one of the reasons we traded Frank. But also, he's going to be vying for Donnie Buford's job. And Donnie Buford did everything for me. But Baylor's coming out of the minor leagues, and you know that you have to keep him, because I'd already sent him down after he was minor league player of the year, the year before. That's how good our organization was at that time. But those are heartbreaking things that eat at you forever and ever and ever. You just don't forget those kinds of things. Telling Brooks, 'I've got to take you out of the lineup'—that still eats at me.

"But as far as that final day in '82, they have great fans in Baltimore. I don't know if we had won that game and gone on to the playoffs and lost, if it would have been the same thing. But naturally, it brings tears to your eyes to know that you were appreciated after all those years. And it was a great ball club. They went on and won the following year. We missed by a game in '82, and the team was still together, and they went on and won in '83—which was fantastic. I wish we'd have won that game. But it's great to know you were appreciated."

Weaver says his job was made easier by the Orioles' scouting department, which, back then, looked not only at a player's athletic prowess, but also at whether he would work hard, be a team player, and not cause too many ripples.

"I had some guys that were hard to handle. But what you try to do is weed them out. And we had a great scouting staff.

Starting in high school, you decide, 'Is this guy going to be a pain in the butt when we sign him, or is he going to be the kind of guy that wants to work and go on to the big leagues, take instructions, and all of that?' That's all scouting. We just had a lot of great guys. One thing about an organization is the fact of longevity. When I went in, I got to set my program. Now, if I'm only going to be there two years, then somebody else has to come in and set a program. If you're only going to be there three years, you'll be getting other people's ballplayers. But I was fortunate enough to stay there 15 years.

"So we signed Bobby Grich the minute Davey Johnson started to slip a little bit. Grich was right there and had learned my way, the things that I want done on cut-offs, relays, everything else. Bobby Grich had learned that right from the day he signed. Everybody does, because we'd bring the minor league managers in and show them what we wanted done during the season. They talked it up to the guys we signed, right from the beginning. Belanger didn't have to do a thing. The minute that we traded Davey Johnson—we had to trade him, to make room for Bobby Grich—it was like Belanger and Grich had played together forever and ever. It was amazing."

Weaver was a master at squeezing the best out of players, at turning role players into vital members of the team, at creating platoons that helped the Orioles to be more than the sum of their parts.

"I appreciate every ballplayer that played for me. Buford is one player whom I especially appreciated. He always got the best out of his ability. There were things I had to do at times. Andy Etchebarren is a great person, but he wasn't hitting too much against right-handers, so we found Elrod [Hendricks]. I found him down in Puerto Rico and talked Baltimore into bringing him up, giving him a chance. And that became a 20-to-25-home run duo, between the two of them. And then there was [Gary] Roenicke and John Lowenstein. I recommended that we get Lowenstein, and we got him for $25,000 on waivers. He was waived all through the league. He played against a lot of right-handers. And Gary Roenicke played against right-handers and left-handers, depending on who was on the mound. But, boy, what a combination. We got more than 35 home runs and about 120 RBIs out of those two guys—in one position. I mean, that's a superstar. Things just fit together greatly."

Weaver took the highly unusual step for a big-league manager of quitting in his prime.

"Managing is not like playing baseball. If I could play today, I'd be out there playing. But managing, like the heartbreak that goes into it and the stress, maybe if I was the type of guy that didn't care if we won or lost, or just had a job, it would have been a different situation. But that's why I went crazy with umpires. Because we have to win. We have to win. I'm that kind of guy. That was my job, and if you don't win, you're going to get fired. That's a cinch. You are going to get fired. I never wanted that to happen to me. Especially after 15 years with one organization—plus the time I spent with them in the minor leagues.

"I didn't want to wear out my welcome. That's another thing. And what you're going to do—I don't care who you are, including me—you're going to wear out your welcome sooner or later, because somebody isn't going to come through for you. I don't care how good a manager you are, that's baseball. The thing about me, all managers do about the same thing. I just was so proud of my baseball judgment to be able to recommend a guy like Lowenstein and get him, because he's a guy that helped us. And along with George Bamberger, my pitching coach, to be able to find a Pat Dobson, who wasn't a .500 pitcher until he got to us and became a 20-game winner. And the same with Steve Stone—a .500 pitcher before, who became a Cy Young Award winner with us.

"We spotted those guys. And we told the organization, 'We've got to have those guys. Go get those guys.' Over the course of the years we lost some guys like a Bobby Grich and Don Baylor through free agency. But you can replace them. And do it cheaper—or kind of cheap. There's nothing cheap any more."

Weaver and his star pitcher, Jim Palmer, loved to do battle with one another. But they also appreciated each other's unique talents. And often, they would go to bat for one another when there was a need.

"In spring training, Palmer—who was going to be my Opening Day pitcher—came to me and told me, 'Look, you've got to go upstairs and tell those guys to renegotiate my contract, or I'm going to have a sore arm on Opening Day.' I went upstairs, and I told the front office. I always stood up for the ballplayers, and I think they appreciated it. But he would have pitched anyway. Everybody was passing Palmer salary-wise. He made a mistake when he signed a two- or three-year contract right at free agency time. But they fixed that. They were fair. The owner was as fair as could be in those days. Jerry [Hoffberger] was kind of a hands-on owner. He'd call us once or twice a month to have lunch downtown, when we were in town, and he wanted a state-of-the-club speech. And Harry Dalton and I, we'd get together and go down and talk to Jerry.

"But only once did he come in to the clubhouse to say anything to me. It was one of those games where we [maybe] got one or two hits the whole game, and probably lost four or five to nothing. And when you get only two hits in a ball game, nothing is happening. It was a bad ball game. And we were on maybe a three-, four-, or five-game losing streak. We very seldom, in those days, lost over three or four in a row. At any rate, after the game, Jerry came bouncing over the rail [from his seats next to the Orioles dugout]. And I heard his footsteps behind me. I didn't want him to say anything in front of the ballplayers. So I walked real fast. And I got in my office, and Jerry came in and slammed the door. He said, 'Earl, I want to tell you something. Tomorrow, I want you to play your best lineup.' I used to have my starting lineup on the front of the card, and all my extra men on the back of the card. I said, 'Jerry, look-it here. There's who played today. Now turn the card over. And look. And tell me who you want in there tomorrow.' And he looked at both sides of the card two or three times. Evidently he realized I had the best guys in there. He looked at me and he said, 'I want to tell you one thing. Make Blair run out to center field.' And it was a fact. Blair struck out three or four times in that ball game.

One was the third out, and he threw the bat over and walked over the mound with his head down. It didn't look good. And by the time the inning was supposed to start, he wasn't even out in center field yet. But Jerry never mentioned anything again about putting different players in the lineup."

CHAPTER 20

Good in a Pinch:
Terry Crowley
(1969-1973; 1976-1982)

The history of Terry Crowley's almost four-decade career in professional baseball is scripted in black and orange. He was signed by the Orioles in 1966, spent four years working his way up the club's minor-league ladder, and finally made the big-league squad at the end of 1969. He played with the Orioles during five of their most successful seasons, spent three years in the National League, and returned to Baltimore for seven more seasons.

After his playing days, he was the Orioles hitting coach from 1985 through 1988. He then worked in the Boston minor-league system and coached at Minnesota for eight years before making his way back to the Orioles as hitting coach in 1999, where he's been ever since.

In the 12 years he was a player with the Orioles, Crowley never had more than 250 at-bats. He was the team's pinch hitter extraordinaire. After the 2006 season, Crowley ranked 12th on all the all-time major-league list for pinch hits, with 108.

He began playing for the Orioles when the team was in its heyday. At that time, there was little turnover on the big-league roster.

"It was really tough to make the Orioles. I came up in the last month of the '69 season, and I went to spring training with the team the next year, coming off a really good Triple-A season. I was young, and I had one of the best springs of my life, and I made the club in '70 as like the 25th man. And that was a wonderful year. There I am breaking in with the team, and we won the division, won the playoffs and won the World Series. It was like, hey, this is the way it's supposed to be. We pretty much had an All-Star at every position [in fact, the Orioles had seven representatives on the American League All-Star squad in 1970, including four starters]. We had a fantastic pitching staff [including three 20-game winners in 1970 and four in 1971]. It was a great time. And that carried on a lot through the '70s. We had really good teams in the 1970s."

Crowley left the Orioles after the 1973 season to play in Cincinnati, and then Atlanta. By the time he returned for his second stint as an Oriole, from 1976 through 1982, baseball had changed forever, and so had the Orioles. Though the Orioles would make it to the World Series again in 1979, the days of a strong nucleus of home-grown players serving as the foundation of the team and remaining in Baltimore year after year were gradually disappearing. Free agency was changing the dynamics of baseball.

"Nineteen seventy-nine was different, because free agency was a lot more a part of things at that time. The Orioles struggled to draw 1.2 million [fans] every year. And our budget wasn't what some teams' budgets were. The Yankees, of course, were leading in attendance, and they had a big budget. It was like a David-and-Goliath type thing. The little guy finally beat the big guy, and all that stuff. Everybody thought of the Orioles as a blue-collar team, hard-working good ballplayers that put in a day's work. And more often than not, we came out on top."

Like most of the Orioles of his era, Crowley took baseball both seriously and with a dose of good humor. The players were

Terry Crowley. *Baltimore Orioles Photos*

confident and deadly serious when it came to winning ball games, but they also had a tremendous amount of fun playing big-league ball. They kept each other loose with pranks and jokes. And teasing your teammates was as much a part of the game as putting on your spikes and uniform.

"Back in the '70s, Merv Rettenmund was my roommate. Merv Rettenmund was one of the funniest, wittiest, sarcastic-type guys that you could ever be around. He was a great teammate. Guys loved him, and he was a really funny guy. In those days, you had maybe just one or two game bats. You had game spikes. You had something else for practice, but you'd save your game spikes for 'The Show'—for game time. The same with batting gloves, etc. So one day we played a 5:30 game in Anaheim. Nolan Ryan was pitching for the Angels. Merv was batting second, and I was batting third. Merv went up to hit. And Nolan blew him away. I mean, boom-boom-boom! Blew him away in three pitches. So I said as we were crossing paths, as I was going up to hit and he was coming back to the dugout, I said to myself, 'Well, here's finally a chance to get this guy who's always so witty and never at a loss for words.' As we crossed paths, I said to him, 'Hey roomy, what's he got?' Merv never hesitated. He said, 'I don't know what he has, but don't take up your game helmet. Because if you do, it's finished.' Because if he hits it, you'll never use it again. He was throwing smoke. You'd think Merv would have said, 'Don't take up your game bat or your game this or that.' But he said, 'Don't take up your game helmet.' That's how overmatched he was in the particular at-bat."

CHAPTER 21

Taking Orders from Jim:
Al Bumbry
(1972-1984)

Al Bumbry came out of the military to play for the Orioles, and from 1972 through 1984, he was more often than not the team's starting center fielder. The club did not always make it to the playoffs during Bumbry's tenure in Baltimore, but the players had confidence and a sense of team. There was continuity on the Orioles, as evidenced by Bumbry's 13 consecutive years on the roster. Known affectionately as "The Bee," he played in one All-Star game as an Oriole, led the team in stolen bases five times and was a consistent hitter atop the lineup, three times batting over .300. But it was winning as a team that meant most to the little left-handed hitter.

"One of the most gratifying aspects of the 12 years I played with the Orioles was that we played in two World Series, and we won a World Series. The big thing is the relationships you build with players when you play together—you win together, you lose together. We had some very good baseball players on our team, but also some very good human beings. There was a confidence that we all felt, come September or October, that we would be in the hunt. In the system under which we operated, with Earl

105

being the manager, the guys knew just what roles they fit into, and how they were going to be used and when they were going to play, etc., etc. We always played as a team, and Earl used all the guys on the club. We didn't have a lot of what you would consider to be superstars. Year in and year out, we weren't picked to finish first and/or second all the time. Several times we were picked to finish fourth or fifth, and we took that as a slap in the face. Earl was constantly on us and driving us and pushing us, that was a major factor also."

Frank Robinson had established an institution in the Orioles clubhouse known as the Kangaroo Court. It was formed as a way for teammates to come together, to judge each other in a humorous way. They cited each other for infractions, both on the field and off, and held court in the clubhouse to decide on guilt or innocence and to assess punishment, usually in the form of a fine. Robinson donned a mop as a wig when he served as judge. The Kangaroo Court continued after Robinson left the team. Bumbry remembers how he once became a reluctant defendant.

"We had them all the time. Elrod, I think, was the court leader, and I think Flanny [Mike Flanagan] or Scottie [McGregor] was, and I think Eddie [Murray] was. A lot of guys were. They were fun. When you screwed up, they'd probably let you know about it. You'd get told about it, and you'd have a chance to defend yourself in court. And when you'd do things good, you'd accumulate some points. And if someone brought you up in court, you'd have a chance to defend yourself.

"Someone brought me up in the court one time for saying it was the bottom of the ninth and there were two outs, and I said, 'Come on, give us this double-play ball.' And someone brought it up in court, 'Bee, there were two outs, we only need one.' So when they brought it up in court, they said, 'How do you plead?' And I said, 'Not guilty.' And they said, 'What do you mean?' And I said, 'Not guilty, because there were two outs, and although I knew we needed only one more out to get out of the inning, I said, 'Come on, give us this double-play ball.' And there's a difference between, 'Come on, let's turn a double play,' and, 'Give us a double-play ball.' 'Give us a double-play ball'—you

Al Bumbry. *Baltimore Orioles Photos*

can get one out to end the inning, and that's what I defended to the hilt. And every time I would say something, they'd slap me with another fine—until I'd used up all the points I had. Then I quit, because I knew I couldn't win. But there was a difference in semantics or terminology when I said, 'Give us a double-play ball.' I didn't say, 'Give us a double play.' They still found me guilty. You couldn't win. And I only protested because I had so many points accumulated. And when I got to the extent of those I'd accumulated, where I'd have to pay a fine, I'd quit. But they were all good. We had good times."

Like so many Orioles, Bumbry took delight in observing the way Weaver and Jim Palmer would butt heads. Both men were headstrong. But sometimes the stubbornness of Weaver or the prima donna air of Palmer would wear off on other players.

"Jimmy always wanted to get in the last word. Earl wanted to get in the last word. Jimmy always wanted to direct traffic when he was out there on the field. I didn't mind so much. He would tell me where to play. He'd turn around on the mound and tell me where to play. Well, I didn't mind when he initially started to do it for the first couple of years. But I guess by the third year, I'd done my homework and played behind him enough that I knew where to play, because I knew how Jimmy pitched, I knew where the hitters usually hit—game situations, stuff like that. Yet Jimmy would still do it. So one day for some reason, I guess I must have been ticked at the world. Well Jimmy stood on the mound, and he kept waving me to the left and waving me to the right, where all these 50,000 people could see. And finally, when I came in, I said, 'Jimmy, look, even if you don't think I know where to play these hitters, don't stand on the mound and tell 50,000 people that I don't know where I'm playing.' Because he never moved Brooks, and he never moved Belanger. But he would move all of us lesser names, so to speak.

"So sure enough, the next inning, Jimmy goes back there on the mound, and he looks back at me, and I can tell he's uncomfortable where I'm playing. He throws a pitch and the guy pops it up, or whatever, and he looks back for the next hitter, and I can tell he doesn't want me where I am. He just turns and looks at the plate, and then he looks back at center. So finally he steps back up on the mound, and instead of facing me, directing me left and right by waving, he stood on the mound and put his hand behind his back and he sort of flipped his fingers telling me where to play. I said, 'OK, all right, Jimmy, what the hell.' At least nobody could see it. But he was good. He knew how he wanted to pitch guys. He knew where they hit the ball. He didn't move Brooksie and Belanger. He tried to move Belanger one time, and Belanger just stood at shortstop and wouldn't move. He'd wave Belanger, and Belanger wouldn't move. Jimmy throws a pitch, and the guy hits a line drive, and Belanger just reaches up and catches it. And Jimmy tips his hat.

"After a while it became funny to watch Jimmy and Earl. After a while you sort of got used to it, and as time went on, it started to irritate you a little bit. But that's just the way they were. Earl wanted to get in the last word. Jimmy wanted to get in the last word. It was one of those kinds of things. It just went back and forth, all the time. There's one thing I can say about Earl. He knew how to push the right buttons. He knew the guys he had to stroke, but he didn't stroke very many guys. He knew the guys to scream at. He knew the guys to leave alone. He screamed at Ed [Eddie Murray] early in Ed's career, and Ed didn't speak to him for three or four months. So from that Earl took it, 'Well, I better leave this guy alone.' And he did."

CHAPTER 22

The Hitting Whiz:
Ken Singleton
(1975-1984)

O utfielder Ken Singleton toiled for five years in the National League with the Mets and Expos before joining the Orioles in 1975. He spent 10 years in Baltimore and carved out a reputation as one of the finest hitters and classiest individuals ever to play for the club.

He led the Orioles in hitting five times, and his .328 average in 1977 is the third highest ever recorded by a Baltimore regular, going into the 2007 season. Now a Yankee broadcaster, Singleton also made the All-Star team five times as an Oriole and is among the top 10 in club history in almost every offensive category—steals being one notable exception. Singleton never was much of a speedster.

He quickly discovered a different attitude from anything he previously had known when he arrived at his first Orioles spring training camp.

"I got traded from Montreal to Baltimore in the winter of '74, so my first year was '75. It was a kind of strange situation up in Montreal, because we weren't that good. We had a team that was either young guys on the way up or old guys that were

Ken Singleton. *Baltimore Orioles Photos*

over the hill. When I came here to Baltimore, the first thing I can recall is the first day I reported to spring training I walked into the locker room and the first person I saw was Brooks Robinson. And right away he put his arm around me and said, 'Here, you don't have to do it all by yourself. We've got other guys who can really play.' And then when I look around the locker room, I saw Mark Belanger, Bobby Grich, Paul Blair, Tommy Davis, and of course Brooksie, and the pitching staff [Mike Cuellar, Jim Palmer, etc.]. I'm thinking, 'He's telling the truth. This is a place I'd like to stay, if I could.' Little did I know I was going to be there for the next 10 years.

"In your career, when people think of you, they think of you as an Oriole. And that's the way I think of myself—as an Oriole. I can recall that very first day in spring training that this place was different from any other team I'd been on. They were very confident, and they knew they could play. And then they just went out and did it."

Singleton also learned that the Orioles of the 1970s and early 1980s were more than just a team—they were a family. There was relatively little turnover on the roster, and the players cared not only about winning, but also about each other. No player personified that attitude more, in Singleton's mind, than the club's great shortstop, Mark Belanger. Singleton remembers "The Blade," an unapologetic smoker who died of lung cancer at the age of 54 in 1998, as a man who cared greatly about his fielding, as well as about his teammates.

"Mark Belanger was going for the record of consecutive errorless games by a shortstop. We were sitting on the airplane heading for Minnesota. He said how much he hated playing in Minnesota. This was before the Metrodome. He said it was the worst infield in the league. He said, 'If I get through here, I'm going to set that record.' The first game, first inning, there was a groundball to short. It goes right through his legs. He looks out to me in right field and waves. All I could do was laugh. And he'd been up in the 80s as far as his errorless streak went. So it kind of went right out the window. I guess he kind of psyched himself out. But he was by far the best fielding shortstop that I've ever seen.

"Mark was the team's player rep, and after he retired, he worked for the union. We were a strong union team. He was very methodical, very organized. You could see why he was such a good fielder. He didn't hit well, but he could play shortstop. And that's primarily what we had him for. When you needed things done, he was the one to talk to. Or if you had any sort of problems, he was the guy to go to. He'd get it fixed. In those days the Orioles trained in Miami, and just about all the players stayed on Key Biscayne. Every spring, he and his wife, Dee, would have a party. You could bring all the members of your family who were down there. My mom used to love those parties. It was like a get-together after a long winter of being away from each other. It kind of got things molded back into a team again. We'd bring wives, single players could bring their girlfriends, your mom and dad, all the kids, there'd be a lot of food, and usually there would be a pool at the house. It was just a big, 'Good to see you again,' sort of thing.

"Being a member of the Orioles was really like being a member of a family. Front office people could come. It was one of those things where we all worked together to win a championship every year. And that was sort of like the kick-off. We're all back together. We've got this purpose. So let's go from here. It was a fun team to be on. And we won a lot of games, that's for sure—which might have made it more fun. The purpose was always there, to win the games—and to enjoy it while you could, too."

Singleton was a hitting whiz in the postseason, batting .333 in American League Championship Series games and .345 in nine World Series games. He played on the team's last World Series team in 1983.

"I think 1983 was more a byproduct of '82 than people give it credit for being. In '82 we came down to the last day of the season, and we were denied by the Brewers. It was a great final series. We had to win all four, and we won the first three, only to fail on the final day. I think for us it really made us tough the next year. We had more injuries in '83 than we had in '82. But I think we were steadfast, and we had the desire to get to the World Series and win a championship, because we were getting older as a team.

"In '79 we got right on the precipice and blew it. We lost to the Pirates. The atmosphere was totally different when we got up, three games to one against Philadelphia [in '83]. There was no celebrating. Everybody was quiet. We knew we had one more game to win. And then Scott McGregor went out and pitched a shutout, and we had won the World Series. But in '79, when we won our third game [to go up against the Pirates, three games to one], it was in come-from-behind fashion. And we were in the clubhouse jumping up and down and yelling, like we had already won. It took me a long time to get over losing that World Series, the reason being that we didn't give the Pirates enough credit. And when they have a player like Willie Stargell on their side, you should give people credit. We didn't do it, and we paid the price."

Singleton credits manager Earl Weaver with helping to keep the team tight as a unit.

"We were so close-knit that you could say anything to anybody. I think, in particular, with Earl, you could yell at him, and you could say things to him that you wouldn't say to other managers. That's primarily because he didn't care about what you said, he just cared about that particular day. I think the good thing about him as a manager was that he would get you to focus on the game at hand. He didn't care about what happened yesterday, or what was going to happen tomorrow. It was what went on today.

"Earl himself might not have been that funny, but the way the players reacted to him was kind of hilarious at times. We kidded him a lot. They were always getting on him because of his height. Whenever he went to the mound to talk to [Jim] Palmer, not necessarily to take him out, but just to talk to him, Earl would come out, and Jim would always get on the top part of the mound to keep Earl well below him."

Catcher Rick Dempsey was another player who contributed to the team in many ways. He wasn't a great hitter, but he helped keep the Orioles both loose and together.

"Rick Dempsey was always a card. The act he portrayed, of Babe Ruth running around the bases, it was just priceless. Those are things that players really don't do today. Maybe it's too businesslike now. When we were in Toronto we had a rain delay, and the Blue Jays offered Rick $5,000 to do his act. He refused to do it. He said, 'I don't do it for money, I just do it for fun.'

"One of the things we did on the team, that people weren't aware of, Rick and I would write out 'Earl's Sons of the Week' list. We'd rank players from one to 25, with one being the best player of the week. Invariably, it always turned out to be Eddie Murray.

No matter what. Because if I had a very good week, I wasn't going to make myself number one. We always made Eddie number one. You'd have that week and the previous week, and you could see how you moved up or went down, according to what we thought your performance was during the week—or how you interacted with Earl. Even Earl would get into this.

"It was funnier when we would release the list on the road. We'd wait until we'd ride on a bus, or ride from the airport to the hotel. There was a captive audience. We read it out loud. And Earl would say, 'That's way too high for him,' or, 'He should be lower, remember he popped up with two men on the other day.' Earl had a good memory for what you did during the week. It was one of those things that helped keep the team together. I bet there was a lot of new guys who would say, 'What is going on here? These guys are having way too much fun.' And we did. We had a lot of fun. If Palmer had an argument with Earl that week, he would always move down on the list. We did that for a couple years in the late '70s, early '80s.

"There was a young man who befriended Rick Dempsey. His name was Ronnie. He was born with a crippling disease. But he was a big Orioles fan. He was about 12 or 13. Rick would bring him into the clubhouse, maybe once every two months. And invariably, we would win that day. And Ronnie would come in with a big smile on his face, and he'd say, 'You guys are the greatest.' You'd see him, barely being able to walk, in a wheelchair on his bad days, and you'd realize that no matter how bad you might be playing, or how bad things might be going, you could be in worse shape. But he was such a big fan that we had Kangaroo Court in his presence. And one day, we decided to trick Ronnie. Ronnie would always bring in cookies or brownies that his mom had baked. We had this picture taken of Tony Armas of Oakland, who used to kill us, eating a brownie. And he signed the picture, 'To Ronnie, thanks for the brownies. That's why I play so well against the Orioles.' So we had this Kangaroo Court, and we bring Ronnie in. Everybody was kind of grumpy towards Ronnie this day. He couldn't understand it. We said, 'Ronnie, you're going to be in Kangaroo Court today.' And Ronnie said, 'What are you talking about?' We said, 'We're bringing you up on charges.' And

Ronnie said, 'Charges of what? I'm the biggest Orioles fan ever.' So Rick brings out this picture signed by Tony Armas eating this brownie, signed to Ronnie, as Exhibit A. And Ronnie's jaw drops. He says, 'I've been framed.' We go through the whole Kangaroo Court deal, and his sentence was, 'You'll be a lifelong member of the Orioles team.' Then we all started laughing, and Ronnie goes, 'Oh, you guys!'

"It was one of those things that was fun to do in those days. And he brightened up our lives. He's long since passed away, but he brought a spirit into the locker room. And he would come in whether we were winning or losing. It didn't matter. He wasn't one of these guys who could come in only when we were on a 10-game winning streak. But when he came in, we'd invariably win. And we always were happy to see him."

The Orioles were a great team during much of Singleton's decade in Baltimore. And they also had their share of characters. Dempsey was one of them. Another was outfielder Benny Ayala.

"Benny Ayala very rarely played defensively, but one day in Minnesota, he was playing left field. He wasn't a very good fielder. That's why he didn't play in the outfield very much. He was primarily a DH. But this one day in Minnesota, he threw two guys out at home plate in one inning. And this guy hadn't been in the field for like a month and a half. So as he comes back into the dugout, he holds his glove up in front of everybody, and he says, 'Look at my glove. It's turning to gold.'"

Singleton was an Oriole when the great Eddie Murray joined the team and supplanted Lee May as the club's first baseman.

"I can recall when Eddie Murray first came up, how quiet he was. Lee May had told Eddie during spring training, 'Rookies don't say anything, they just play.' So Eddie follows this to the tee. He never said anything to anybody. So Earl, after about a week into the season, comes up to Lee May and says, 'Does this guy like me? He hasn't said anything to me.' And Lee said, 'Oh, yeah, he likes you. He told me.'

"Pat Kelly and Lee were standing in the outfield during Eddie's first batting practice session in spring training the year he first came up. And he's hitting balls over the wall left-handed and right-handed. And they didn't know who he was. Pat said, 'Who is this guy?' And Lee said, 'Some rookie.' And Pat says, 'I don't even know what position he plays.' So they're standing out there, and Pat says, 'Let's see where he goes after he hits. Let's see what kind of glove he picks up.' So after Eddie hits 10 balls out of the stadium, he goes back to the dugout, gets his glove and goes over to first base. And Pat Kelly says, 'Oh, Lee. You're in trouble.'"

Like all Orioles from the Weaver days, Singleton remembers how the gritty little manager would often get on the nerves of his players—even the best of them.

"Paul Blair was probably the best center fielder of his era. He won eight Gold Gloves. One day we were in Minnesota, and somebody happened to hit a ball over his head. When he came back to the dugout, Earl was steaming. He couldn't wait for the inning to be over. He yelled at Blair, 'I don't want to ever see a ball go over your head again for the rest of your career.' Nobody likes to be yelled at in front of everybody, particularly after you've already won six Gold Gloves. And Blair is noted for playing shallow. So I go out to my position in right field the next inning, and I look over and I don't see Blair. I look again, and he's standing on the warning track, with his arms folded. And he's really mad. From the dugout, they're waving towels, trying to get him to move. And he wouldn't move in. Fortunately during the inning, nothing was hit toward him. After the inning's over, we go back into the dugout, and Earl goes, 'Oh, go ahead and play where you want to play.'"

CHAPTER 23

The Call:
Mike Flanagan
(1975-1987; 1991-1992)

M ike Flanagan, now the Orioles executive vice president of baseball operations, was one of the best left-handed starters in team history. He also was one of the wittiest men ever to wear the Baltimore uniform. Anyone who ever played with Flanagan marvels at how funny he was and how adept he was with the one-liner. He was even more skillful, though, with his pitching arm. Flanagan won the American League Cy Young Award in 1979, after going 23-9. He pitched in two World Series with the Orioles and notched 141 victories for the team—the fifth most in club history.

Although he was a starter almost his entire career, he moved to the bullpen in 1991 and pitched one of the most memorable games in team history as a reliever. It was on Sunday, October 6, 1991, the Orioles' final game in old Memorial Stadium. The game culminated a nostalgic weekend series against the Tigers. Though the Orioles had announced that a special ceremony would be held after the final game that Sunday, almost no one, including Flanagan, knew precisely what would be taking place. Almost every great player in team history, as well as dozens of the

Mike Flanagan. *Baltimore Orioles Photos*

not so great ones, were invited to take the field after the game and stand at the position where they played for the team. It was an incredibly moving event, and the emotion that accompanied the knowledge that the old stadium on 33rd Street's final baseball game was being played that day left few in the crowd of 50,700—not to mention the players themselves—tearless.

Flanagan was the true-blue Orioles veteran of the 1991 team, beloved by fans and teammates alike, and he dearly hoped to pitch in the final game.

"Going into the final weekend, I had the feeling that something special was going to be happening. The PR department was very secretive about the plans, but I think we all knew something special was going to take place—and maybe myself more than anyone else on that team, as far as the players were concerned. I felt the importance of having everything going out the right way. It was such an important place—Memorial Stadium—to all of us. My best years certainly were on that field; [it was] just the same for many others who were coming back for that weekend. So I sort of felt the weight of it all, and there was talk of certainly my pitching in the last game, but I wasn't sure about being the last one out there.

"[The final night game in Memorial Stadium history] started on Friday. I pitched in Friday's game, and my routine for the whole year was pretty much pitching in every other game. I had a lot of appearances that year and was very proud of that fact. I was close to Tippy Martinez's team mark for appearances by left-handed pitchers. I needed, I think, three to break his record, which would have been very satisfying for me because it was the first year ever for me in the bullpen after spending years in the starting rotation. So it was something for me to pin the season on.

"So I pitched in Friday's game, and there was a situation in Saturday's game in which I normally would have been in. And I didn't get the call. So I started getting the feeling that there was a plan, that I was maybe purposely held out of that game to pitch on Sunday. So I really didn't know what to expect. I can remember getting up Sunday morning and starting to feel the weight of the day—'This is the last time I'm ever going to drive this way to this ballpark.' It was different than the seventh game of a World Series. In some ways, it was bigger than that. The fans were at the ballpark, and the place was buzzing like a World Series game. It was kind of confusing. The day had everything. John Unitas and Brooks Robinson were out on the field. It was like the old days. I was very proud at that point to still be playing, to have been multi-generational, to have played with Brooksie, to still be there participating, and being able to have a hand in it.

"Bob Milacki started, and I remember the game didn't go well early. The Tigers were pretty much ready to go home for the end of the season, but there was electricity in the air. Even some players on our team had made their travel arrangements and were ready to go home, but I didn't want it to end. I didn't want it to change.

"I can remember taking a stroll under the left-field stands. They had a restroom back there. I remember looking in the mirror about the fourth or fifth inning and saying, 'This is really going to happen.' I really started feeling the weight of the occasion. The things I always preached as pitching coach—'You don't let the can'ts and don'ts and what-ifs get in the way of your thinking, because a lot of times you'll create a negative snowball—so I just went in there and looked in the mirror and gave myself a lecture that this was going to happen. My worst nightmare was, 'What if you come in and they get seven straight hits and five runs and everybody's going to be horrified?' So I had to literally go in there and push those thoughts out of my mind and give myself a lecture.

"As the game proceeded, Gregg Olson got up to warm up. I still wasn't sure what was going to take place. Nobody came to me and said, 'You've got the last outs.' The game was going on, but things felt a little different because Olson [the team's closer] never went in games before I did. He was always after me. He went out to start the ninth inning, and then I got the call to warm up. And I asked Elrod [Hendricks] if he would warm me up one more time. Elrod had been my first catcher in the big leagues, we [later] coached together, we'd been through most of the wars together. He'd had a bad back for most of the second half of the season, so he didn't do a lot of catching in the pen. But I asked if he'd warm me up one more time. So he did. After Olson got the first out, Johnny Oates went to the mound, and I thought, 'This is going to happen.' I got the call, and I remember coming around the fence and heading into the ballpark. Most times I would run in from the bullpen. This time I almost felt like a rookie again, I was afraid I was going to fall down if I ran. So I took my time going in and allowed the tension and the drama to build up.

"Bob Melvin was the catcher, and he and Johnny Oates were on the mound. I can still see him standing there. Melvin had his arm on his hip and said to me, 'God, that took a long time.' And he handed me that ball and said, 'Let's go.' I'll never forget the song they played over the loudspeaker. It was, 'You've Got to Have Heart.' The place was completely involved.

"It was almost one of those things—pitchers talk about getting into the zone, or whatever—my concentration level was as good as it had ever been in any game. And most times in the past it was easy to diffuse the pressure by saying, 'Well, it's us against them.' There was always a way to diffuse the pressure from it being an individual moment. You could always make it a team moment, not an individual one. But this time I couldn't find any of those reasons, which made it very difficult to proceed. I was facing a couple of hitters—Dave Bergman was a player that I played against in the minor leagues and winter ball, and he was the first hitter. I went to three-and-two on him and threw another curve ball, and he had this wrap-around swing for strike three. The moment was still building. And Travis Fryman was the next hitter. He came up, and I remember falling behind early in the count. And then there was a two-and-two pitch, I think, I threw a curve ball that I thought ended up right down the middle of the plate. And the umpire called it a ball. So the thought that went through my mind was, 'You've been playing for 19 years, and the stadium's closing, you'd think if you'd ever get a break on a pitch, this would be the one.' But he called it ball three. And I came back and threw another curve ball, almost identical, and he swung and missed. And that was the final out. I got a chill. There was the gamut of emotions. Bob Melvin gave me the baseball, and I clung to it very tightly as a very cherished item. And I never was that way about things. But that ball meant everything.

"And I just remember tearing up. I walked off the field and was going down into the tunnel, and again, not knowing what was planned for the ceremonies, I was walking back to the clubhouse and there were Frank and Brooks and Boog and Palmer and Cuellar. The generations were all lined up in the hallway. It was an amazing moment in the bowels of that stadium just to see the generations of great players that had been there. I felt really fortunate just to get through it. And I'd felt like I'd done it for those guys in the hallway, at least to give them a good moment, a final moment, that they could remember and I could remember and carry forever. It really did work out wonderfully well."

CHAPTER 24

No. 1 Pick:
Rich Dauer
(1976-1985)

Rich Dauer's entire big-league career was spent with the Orioles, from 1976 through 1985. He started at second base for the team during most of those years, and teamed with Cal Ripken Jr. for the Orioles' keystone combination during Ripken's first few years at shortstop with the club.

When the Orioles signed Dauer, he had just come off two national championship collegiate teams at Southern Cal. In his senior year, he was named All-America. He rightfully thought he was a pretty hot commodity, but it didn't take Dauer long to get his comeuppance, at the hands of Cal Ripken Sr. Senior was Dauer's first minor-league manager and one of the key architects of The Oriole Way—the club's legendary formula for success at both the major- and minor-league levels, based on the simplest of ingredients: sound, fundamental baseball and a winning attitude.

"I remember the very first day I came to the Orioles organization. I was the No. 1 pick out of USC. It was in Asheville, North Carolina, in 1974. I went right from college to Double-A.

Rich Dauer. *Baltimore Orioles Photos*

I walked into the clubhouse and Cal Ripken Sr. was the manager. He just grabbed me around the throat, and he threw me up against the wall. He said, 'Hey, I don't care who you are or what you did in college. This is a team. This is the Orioles, and you're one of us now. If you give me 110 percent, I don't care if you hit .300 or whatever. As long as you give me 110 percent, I'll be happy and we'll get along fine.'

"I believe that was the beginning of The Oriole Way—The Ripken Way. It was major intimidation. Obviously, the Ripken family hadn't become the Ripken family yet.

"When you went to USC, we thought we were really good, because we won championship after championship. It was like the Yankees of college baseball. The best players would always go or migrate to USC at that time [as Dauer himself did, transferring from San Bernardino Valley College]. I was fortunate to go there, and I was fortunate to be picked No. 1 by the Orioles. I thought I was just going to go there and take the world by storm. I found out differently, real quick."

After Cal Sr., Dauer got to experience what it was like playing under Earl Weaver in Baltimore. Weaver could be infuriating to play for, but the players put up with his cantankerous ways because he was smart and he was a winner. And despite Weaver's reputation for being a real tough manager, the players found ways to humor and tease him. As much as Weaver could dish it out, the players would throw it right back at him.

"We used to have a lot of fun with Earl. He was so into the game. On every pitch he would be jumping. He had his little thing he'd do to try to get you to play well. He'd say things like, 'Please, get a base hit.' The greatest thing about our team, though, was that we had such a great bunch of guys that we were always kidding around and joking around on the bench during the game. When we were out on the field, the game didn't just stop there. If I was sitting on the bench, which, unfortunately, I did quite a bit, especially in the early part of my career and at the end of my career, you were still into the game and involved. We used to play pranks on each other.

"Earl would have the habit of smoking. And you weren't allowed to smoke in the dugout. In order to do that, you had to hide. He would run back into the corner sometimes and light up a cigarette. There was an old friend of his, Ron Luciano, who was an umpire. For some reason, they just didn't see eye to eye. Well, I guess Earl didn't see eye to eye with anybody—he had to look up to everybody [because he was pint-sized]. He and Ron didn't get along real well. When Earl would go back and light a cigarette, the pitch would be thrown by our pitcher, and it would be high and outside. And we'd start screaming, 'Hey, Earl, Ron's screwing us again. It's right down the middle, and he called it a ball.' So Earl would run back out, and he'd say to Luciano, 'Hey, you idiot, where was that pitch?' Then he'd go back and finish his cigarette. And the next pitch would come, and it was low and in the dirt. And we'd go, 'Earl, he just missed another one.' And he'd come flying out of the dugout again, yelling at Ron.

"We'd use Earl to our advantage. But it was also an honor to play for him. The more I'm involved in baseball [before becoming the Colorado Rockies minor-league infield coordinator, Dauer spent time as a Milwaukee Brewers bench coach and Kansas City Royals third-base coach] and around a lot of people, the more I realize how fortunate I was to be around such a great manager."

Dauer got to play on two World Series teams with the Orioles, in 1979 and 1983. He and other players on those two teams remember how the hallmark of both clubs was the sense of team and togetherness.

"We had a lot of memorable games in '83. There was always somebody different to help us win a game. We were such a team, we were such a bunch of guys, that we didn't really care who did the job, as long as we won the game. It was so important for us to play together as a unit. I remember a lot of times, just the fun of coming back and never thinking that we were ever going to lose. It was just a really special year.

"I'll always remember hitting a home run to win Earl Weaver Day. Of all the people to come through and win a game for him to be me would have probably been everybody's last choice. That was a thrill. And making it even more so, it was Mike Flanagan's 100th win. So two milestones that are quite important to Mike and to Earl also are very special to me."

CHAPTER 25

Baltimore's Own "Babe Ruth": Rick Dempsey
(1976-1986; 1992)

Rick Dempsey always has been a fan favorite in Baltimore, during his playing days as a catcher with the Orioles and more recently as the team's first-base coach. He was one of those rare players who loved to entertain the fans. Perhaps his most famous routine was his imitation of Babe Ruth calling his legendary home run shot in the World Series against the Chicago Cubs. Dempsey would perform this act on the tarpaulin during rain delays and conclude it by rounding the bases and comically sliding into home, sometimes splashing into the plate amidst puddles and a driving rain. Dempsey's performance was inspired by a former Yankee teammate before the catcher joined the Orioles for the first of his 12 seasons as an Orioles catcher.

"When I was with the New York Yankees in 1976, we had a relief pitcher named Sparky Lyle. He used to get the balls from the outfield in batting practice. He would make one section in the stands scream louder for it, and then he'd throw them a ball. He got the fans involved in the game, looking for souvenirs. He said one time he wanted to do this Babe Ruth pantomime, where

Rick Dempsey. *Baltimore Orioles Photos*

he'd run around the bases on the tarp. So that's what gave me the idea. I heard it from Sparky Lyle first.

"Then, in 1977, when I was with the Orioles, it got down to the last week of the season, we were tied with the Boston Red Sox, both of us two games back. So the pennant race was over with. It was raining that day in Boston. We were taking batting practice, and I was doing the same thing Sparky would do. I'd get one section to scream louder, and I'd throw them a ball. It started to rain when we were leaving batting practice, and there was one ball left out on the tarp after they pulled the tarp out onto the field. I thought, 'Well, hell, I'll go out and get that one ball, and I'll get one section to scream louder than the other.' But as I got out there I couldn't walk. I started sliding. So I skated over to the ball. And as I was skating toward the ball, the organist started playing, 'Raindrops keep Falling on My Head. So I just got to leading the fans in a little song. Everybody started singing. So I skated around for a while, and then I threw the baseball in the stands, and I left the field.

"I went back into the dugout. And I was sitting, actually, in the men's room, and I started to hear the fans beating on the roof of the stadium there. And it's deafening when you're underneath the grandstand in Boston. They started beating real loud, and I was wondering what the commotion was. Then Richie Dauer came running in and said, 'Demper, they want you to come back out.' I didn't know what to do. And then the thought came to me again to do the Babe Ruth pantomime. So I went out there, and I did the pantomime of Babe Ruth calling his home run, swinging and then running around the bases, and sliding in from third base to home. And that's how it all began.

"After that, every time it would get cloudy and start to rain in stadiums, general managers would call me up and ask me if I'd do it. In Toronto once they asked me to do it. I looked up in the stands and there were about 10 people there. So I said no. I did it again in Baltimore, and the second time I did it was in Milwaukee. I did a pantomime, not of Babe Ruth hitting a home run, but of Robin Yount hitting two home runs on the last day of the season to beat us in 1982.

"My father was a vaudevillian, but it really had nothing to do with my pantomimes. He did the 'Song of Norway' on Broadway in New York. He was a singer also. He had some thespian in him, I guess."

Another source of amusement for Dempsey—as well as for all his teammates—was the behavior of manager Earl Weaver.

"When Pat Kelly was on the ball club, we had a game against Minnesota. Larry Hisle was the big RBI producer in the league at that time. The day before, we were in Chicago. Brooks Robinson was still with the ball club. Earl Weaver was coming out to bring a new pitcher in. And he didn't really notice that a right-handed hitter was coming up. He thought there was a left-handed hitter. He had told me to walk the hitter before. And then he came out to bring [left-hander] Tippy [Martinez] in. So he brought [Tippy] in, but he didn't realize there was a right-hander hitting. So I told him, 'Earl, there's a right-hander up, why are you bringing Tippy in?' Then he looked back, and then he looked at Brooks, and he said to Brooks, 'You know every time I talk to this guy, he confuses me. He confuses me.' So he made the mistake of bringing Tippy in to face a right-hander. On the way back, he told me never to say anything to him again, that I confused him.

"So the next game was at home against Minnesota, and Larry Hisle was coming up. And Dan Ford was on the same Minnesota ball club at that time, too. Dan Ford was coming up with men on second and third. And Earl wanted me to walk Dan Ford to get to Larry Hisle. And Larry Hisle was leading the league in hitting and RBIs. So I looked over at Earl, and I was wondering what he was doing. I looked back at him, and I kept trying to get his attention, without saying anything. But he didn't pick up on it. He kept saying, 'Put him on.' So, okay. Ball one. Ball two. Ball three. And then finally, Pat Kelly said, 'Why are you walking Dan Ford?' And Earl goes, 'That's not Dan Ford. That's Larry Hisle.' And Pat goes, 'No, Larry Hisle's on deck.' And just as we're throwing ball four, Earl tries to yell and scream, 'Don't walk him. Don't walk him.' But it was too late, and we ended up walking him. Hisle comes up to bat, and he gets an infield hit. And they end up beating us, 2-1, on that play.

"Weaver was screaming and hollering when I came back to the dugout, 'Jiminy Christmas! Why didn't you tell me? Why didn't you tell me?' I said, 'Well, you just got through telling me yesterday not to say anything to you ever again.' Pat Kelly was sitting there on the bench, and I remember Earl going down the bench. He said to Pat, 'Well, they all look alike.' [Kelly, like both Hisle and Ford, is African-American.] And Pat Kelly went crazy. He knew Earl had made a political faux pas there. He didn't really mean to say it like that, and Pat Kelly just killed him."

Dempsey and Weaver might have had their moments, but the real explosions came when Weaver and his star pitcher, Jim Palmer, went at it on the mound. And Dempsey, as the Orioles' catcher, had the best seat in the house for the Weaver and Palmer brouhahas.

"They used to have the best battles out on the mound that I have ever heard. Earl would come out on the mound and say to Jim, 'What are you doing? How are you pitching these guys? You're not pitching them right.' I would go to the front of the mound. And then when they'd start to get mad at each other, and start yelling back and forth at each other, they'd have the best lines. Earl would say he didn't know what he was doing out there pitching. And Palmer would fire back, 'The only thing you knew about pitching is that you couldn't hit it.' Oh, they'd get so mad. And at that point, it was time for me to leave. It was so funny, because Earl would get so mad at him. But Palmer would just fire back at him with little quips."

Dempsey was certainly a thespian himself on the field, but he also contributed mightily to the Orioles' success over the years, especially during the postseason. Though never a strong hitter, Dempsey batted .400 in two league championship games with Baltimore. He also batted .286 in the 1979 World Series against Pittsburgh. And in October of 1983, he had his greatest moment of glory, batting .385 with a home run and winning the most valuable player award in the World Series against the Phillies. One at-bat in that Series also changed Dempsey's career.

"I was hitting ninth. But one thing I noticed, in the second game of the 1983 World Series, I was getting pitched pretty much the same way every single time up. They'd start me off with a fastball away, then a breaking ball, then another fastball. And then they'd come in with the breaking ball, on two balls and one strike. It was the same routine—away and in, away and in. So in the second game of the World Series, Charlie Hudson's third pitch was away again, and I took a fastball down the right-field line, which is something I hadn't done in a long time. I hit it off the wall, and the go-ahead run scored. That was like a changing point for me in my career. I distinctly remember that as the at-bat that really set up the second half of my whole career. I felt like a 2,000-pound weight fell off my back at that point. Because I had driven in the go-ahead run in Game 2, and I had done something offensively to help the ball club. I just relaxed so much from that point on. I wasn't afraid to make an out any more, and I just let the natural ability take over. I didn't hit high for averages any more, but I was a productive hitter for the rest of my career, for the last 12 years of my major-league career.

"The rest of that World Series, I never had a single. Everything was doubles and a home run. It just seemed like the ball looked like a basketball to me up there. It wasn't a big offensive Series, because Eddie [Murray] and Cal [Ripken] didn't get going until the last game. Eddie finally hit two home runs then. I figured if the Series had gone six or seven ball games, Eddie Murray probably would have been the MVP. And they pitched Cal tough that entire Series. He just didn't get a lot of good pitches to hit. So it just got down to me, and it seemed like I was the guy that set up the innings. I didn't drive in a lot of runs, but I just got good pitches to hit, and I hit them in spots where nobody caught them. I did most of my hitting in Philadelphia. Memorial Stadium was a very tough ballpark for me to hit in. The corners were cut, and it forced the outfielders to give you the lines and bunch you in the gap. I couldn't hit the ball out of the ballpark, so anything I hit in the gap would always get run down. I had a tough time hitting in that ballpark, but I hit fairly well away from Baltimore. I'd probably have been a much better hitter if I'd grown up in a different stadium. But I hit well in Philly down the lines, and I hit my home run in the gap. And that was it.

"The pitching was outstanding in that Series. Our relief pitching was great—Tippy and Sammy Stewart were awesome.

They just closed the door every single time out. Scottie McGregor pitched two good ball games. He lost, 2-1, and then he pitched the final game and won, 5-0.

"Winning the Series MVP Award was one of those things that kind of snuck up on me. In my last at-bat of the last game, I started thinking, 'You know, I might get an MVP if we can win this game. We had a comfortable lead, 5-0. And then I started thinking about all that stuff, like, 'Hey, I'm probably in contention.' And then as soon as the game was over, before I even left the field, some writer yelled at me and said, 'You got the MVP.' I was pretty elated. Winning the World Series, and then getting the MVP. It was something I wasn't thinking about at any time, up until then."

CHAPTER 26

A Game for the Record Books: Tippy Martinez
(1976-1986)

As a left-handed pitcher for the Orioles from 1976 through 1986, Tippy Martinez was one of the greatest relievers in club history. He is second to Gregg Olson among all-time save leaders for the Orioles. In the 1983 World Series against the Phillies, he picked up saves in two of the club's four victories. For six of the 11 years he was with Baltimore, the tiny Martinez and the hulking right-hander Tim Stoddard formed a formidable duo in the Orioles' bullpen.

Despite his many great accomplishments as an Oriole, Martinez will be remembered primarily for one incredible outing. On August 24, 1983, against the Toronto Blue Jays, Martinez came in in relief with none out in the 10th inning and retired the side by picking three runners off first base. It's a feat never accomplished by any other big-league pitcher.

The game was memorable for many reasons. The Orioles had tied it up in the bottom of the ninth after trailing by two runs with two outs. The Jays had taken a lead on a Cliff Johnson home run in the top of the 10th, before Martinez entered the game. And after he held them scoreless for the rest of the inning, Cal Ripken

Jr., who was celebrating a birthday that day, hit a home run to tie it. And then little Lenn Sakata bashed a three-run homer to win the amazing game for the Orioles.

"We were in a tense competition with Toronto at the time, fighting for our division. It was a seesaw battle with Toronto in that particular game, going back and forth. I came into the game for Stoddard, and there was a runner on first base, Barry Bonnell. At that time Earl had gone through all his roster, so he had to make roster moves. We had [infielder] Lenn Sakata catching, who'd never caught before, other than in high school. We had [outfielder] Gary Roenicke, who'd never played third base before in his life, at third. I had the agile [outfielder] John Lowenstein playing second base. He had probably no range at all. And we had Eddie [Murray] at first base, and at shortstop was Cal.

"And we had these Toronto runners, who were so anxious to run, because they knew they could steal. Lenn Sakata had not been playing a whole lot, so when he got into the game, he thought, 'Maybe this would be an opportunity to show Earl that I could catch a little bit' at my expense. When we were on the mound, Lenn said, 'Why don't you give me an opportunity to see if I could throw this guy out?' I said, 'No, I don't think so. I don't think so.' Then he asked, 'Do you want to throw curve balls?' I said, 'Are you kidding? You won't catch this guy.' So I had to throw all fastballs, on the outer part of the plate.

"It just so happened that little things come back to you—what we called 'little field,' that we used when we trained in Miami. Little field are the techniques we used in learning how to do certain things with runners on base, and what have you. It's more or less trying to define a better move to first base. And it just all came together with the runners being anxious to run on Sakata and myself, in combination with having a decent move. It all kind of played together.

"So I picked Bonnell off. And the next guy, Dave Collins, got an infield hit through Lowenstein, who had that terrific range. So Dave Collins, who was a speedster, was at first base. So I thought, 'Oh, my gosh, what am I going to do here?' I gave him a dummy move to first base, and then I went back again and gave him one of my better moves, and picked him off.

Tippy Martinez. *Baltimore Orioles Photos*

"In the meantime, [Toronto manager] Bobby Cox was in the dugout, and I could see him just hollering and screaming and kicking the water cooler and denting the thing. He was just going nuts. He was telling his first base coach, 'If anybody gets on, I don't want them an inch off first base.' And it just so happened I walked the left-handed hitter, Willie Upshaw. And he wasn't even a foot off—maybe half a foot—off the bag. And it just so happened, it was a habit at the time, I gave him another dummy move and went over to first base. Actually, I did it twice. And the third time, I gave him one of my better moves, I guess. It just really clicked, and wouldn't you know it, I picked the guy off first base as well. And the fans just went nuts. I mean, it just kind of sparked us. I knew that getting out of that inning was a big key for us. But also I knew we couldn't sustain another inning with those guys in the infield. They did not have experience at those positions. Somebody would have had to have been the goat for us, and I just didn't want to be that goat. We had to do something. We were down by a run. And it just so happened we got two runners on in the bottom of the inning, and Lenn comes up and hits a three-run homer. And he wins the ballgame. The fans just went wild."

Like many Orioles pitchers of that day, Martinez often found himself in a position where he disagreed with Weaver on a particular strategy. And sometimes, when he thought Weaver was clearly wrong, Martinez ignored what his manager told him to do.

"We were in Cleveland, and we were winning by two or three runs. We had a space open at first base to walk a guy, or I could have pitched to him. Earl tells me to throw to the guy. He calls it a challenge. I forget who the batter was, but Earl wanted me to throw all fastballs to him and no breaking balls. Well, my best pitch was my breaking ball. I said, 'Earl, I can get him on a breaking ball.' And he goes, 'Your instructions are to throw him all fastballs.' I just looked at [catcher] Rick [Dempsey], and Rick had this blah kind of look, this dull look, like, 'We're not going to do this. We're going to throw breaking balls.' Earl goes back, and he's expecting me to throw fastballs. On my first pitch, Rick throws down a two, which is the call for a breaking ball. So I threw it for a strike. And Earl stood up in the dugout and did the old, famous whistle that he does, and whistled to Rick. He throws his hands up. Rick and I look at each other. So we threw another one. And we threw another one and struck the guy out. And Earl was happy about it, as far as the results of it, but he couldn't believe that we did that."

That wasn't the only time Martinez and Weaver didn't see eye to eye.

"We were in Oakland, and Jim Palmer was starting the game. Before the game, I went into Earl's office to complain about him taking me out of games after I did all the horse work. I wanted to get the saves. Needless to say, there was some screaming and shouting. The clubhouse got kind of quiet, because people wanted to listen to what was going on. The last thing that came out of Earl's mouth was, 'Martinez, when we get back home after this game, you're out of here. I'm trading your ass.' I told him I couldn't wait to go. So Palmer starts the game, and they score five or six runs off him in the first inning, and he gets one out. Well, Earl decides he wants to punish me. I was the short reliever, and sometimes the middle reliever, but this day he puts me in the game in the first inning. I go into the game and throw 8 $^2/_3$ innings of no-hit ball. And we come back and win the game. We come in, and everybody's happy, we're having a whole happy party, and Earl sticks his head out into the clubhouse. He says, 'Hey, Martinez, when we get back home, you're not going anywhere.'

"Everyone knows of the feuds between Palmer and Earl. But it's really been with a lot of guys. The big thing with me always was when Earl would take me out of games. He once made the statement to me, 'You know, Tip, you're the worst left-hander the Orioles have ever had in the history of this franchise.' And I told him, 'Earl, you're the worst manager I've had in my whole career.' So we kind of left it on that note for a couple of years. Then they had a big party when he retired. I can remember getting a few hors d'oeuvres and what have you, and Earl called me over to the side. He said, 'You know, Tip, you're one of the best left-handers I've ever had.' Of course, he was sober at the time, I guess. And I said, 'You know what, Earl, you're one of the best managers I've ever had.' So, I guess things do work out, somehow and some way. But he was a manager who had a lot of drive to get players to play his way. It's either his way or the highway. That's just the way it was.

"Earl had a contentious relationship with most of his players. I had a talk with Rick Dempsey, because Rick would always have confrontations with him. I said, 'Rick, I can't get through to this man. He doesn't listen to me.' Rick says, 'You've got to go in there, and you've got to holler at him. He's going to talk over you because he can scream louder than you can. That's obvious. He does it with everybody. But he likes that. So you've got to scream, and you've got to fight for what you believe in.' So I did. And wouldn't you know it, every time that I did go in there and argue with him, I'd pitch longer. He kept me in more games, and I'd stay in longer. But if you wanted somebody on your side, he was definitely for the players, as far as negotiations or things like that, like working on a bonus and you needed so many innings."

One day the Orioles were playing at Kansas City, and the Royals were stealing bases at a record-setting pace. The primary victim was Mike Flanagan, the team's resident wit and star left-hander. Martinez remembers that Dempsey was unhappy because his percentage of runners thrown out went way down that day, so he complained to Weaver.

"Rick told Earl, 'I can't throw anybody out, because your pitchers can't keep anybody close to the bag.' After the game we had a special meeting. We were on the way back to Baltimore on the plane from Kansas City. And we were scheduled for a day off. And we cherish our days off. But we were told on the plane that because of what happened in Kansas City, all the pitchers had to go to the stadium on the off day to have a special practice with Rick, on keeping runners close to first base.

"We were all by the mound, and Earl said that somebody had to go on the mound. Mike decided that he better be the one, because we were there because of him. So Earl told Rick to get behind the plate and catch the ball Mike would throw. And then he said, 'I'm going to be on first base. I'm going to be the runner.' So here's this guy on first, this short little guy with high socks. He looked like a midget, leading off first base. So Earl took this lead—oh, gosh—it was so big you wouldn't think of doing it in a game, it was almost half way. He said, 'I want to prove a point.' He said, 'Just keep me still, don't give me any kind of a starting run, and see if Rick can throw me out.' Of course, Mike can throw a blazing fastball. But he threw a mediocre fastball to home, Rick comes up gunning, and he throws the ball to second. A bam-bam play. Well, Earl slides. He slides the whole nine yards, and they tag him out. So he goes, 'Okay!' Then we all go back to the dugout.

"And Earl says, 'Okay, guys, you saw what happened. Did anybody learn anything from this?' because Earl wanted to get out of there, too. He didn't want to have us spend the day practicing on our day off. So after Earl asked, Mike, as witty as he is, thought about it for a second. And Mike says, 'We're not giving the runners a big enough lead?' Earl threw his hands up and everything. He couldn't believe it. But we understood what he was trying to do."

Martinez was primarily a breaking ball pitcher, and his bullpen colleague, Stoddard, was a fastball pitcher. But one day out in the bullpen, their roles seemingly were reversed.

"We were in Texas, and in Texas, the fans can literally touch you. That's how close the fans were to the bullpen. We were throwing, and it just so happened we had double-barrel throwing in the bullpen, a left-hander and a right-hander, getting ready to go into the game. It was Tim Stoddard and myself. I felt I was throwing exceptionally well, everything was together at the time. I was getting the glove to pop, it was loud, and all the fans were turning to look. They were saying, 'Who the heck is throwing?' Every time I threw the ball, the glove would just pop like crazy. Elrod was catching Tim. And one of the fans said, 'Hey look, there's David and Goliath.' Tim's 6-foot-7, and I'm 5-foot-10—but I'm really 5-foot-9—maybe. So I'm popping the glove, and every time Stoddard threw, it was like a powder-puff ball. It didn't do anything.

"Some fan came out there, and he was so loud. Sometimes you get one fan who's so loud, you can just hear it. He says, 'Look, it's David and Goliath, and the little guy is throwing harder than the big guy.' So Tim got so pissed. He was grunting and trying to throw his fastball through the catcher. He just couldn't do it. He didn't have it that particular day. That was so funny to me.

"In the bullpen, we had a good chemistry. We were serious about the game, but we also could have fun."

CHAPTER 27

A Tip of the Cap to the Skipper:
Steve Stone
(1979-1981)

Steve Stone was a 31-year-old right-hander when he came to the Orioles from the White Sox in 1979. He pitched for the Orioles for only three years. He was 11-7 in his first season in Baltimore for a team that made it to the World Series. And in 1980, Stone went 25-7, earning more victories than any other pitcher in club history.

He credits much of his success while in Baltimore to the team's strong bullpen and the organization's winning culture.

"I think I was very fortunate to get to the Orioles at a time in their history when everything pretty much came together. It was a group of guys that understood what it took to win. For me it was one of those enchanted years where just about everything went right. I remember from [beginning the 1980 season] 2-3, I won 14 straight games, then lost one in Texas, then won five in a row after that. But it was a year that saw the bullpen save every game I left with the lead until my last game of the year. Then there were two outs in the ninth inning, and I think it was Tim Stoddard who gave up a double that scored a run to Joe Charboneau, who went on to be the Rookie of the Year. But when you have a year when the bullpen saves every game that you leave, you know that it's going to be a special season. And it was for me. If I gave up four, we scored five. Whatever I had to have happen, they were able to do it. They turned huge double plays when they had to. It was a team, when you put it down on paper and compared it to the New York Yankees of that era, or the Boston Red Sox, this is a team that probably shouldn't have won. But as a team, we were just a little bit better than those other teams.

"I remember going to Milwaukee, and walking up the runway after the Brewers scored 23 runs against us in a three-game series. I didn't pitch in it…and as I'm walking up the runway I was next to Mark Belanger. I was new to the team. It was 1979. I remember shaking my head, and Belanger goes, 'What are you concerned about?' I said, 'Well, 23 runs in three games, Mark. That was just awful.' And he goes, 'You mean that?' He goes, 'Oh, no. We come here twice more. We come here toward the end of June, the beginning of July.' And he says, 'We come here the beginning of September.' And he said, 'You have to understand something about the Orioles. And that is, after June 1, nobody hits our pitching. Nobody! So when we come back, we'll kill that team.' And that's exactly what happened."

Stone found that it took a little bit of time—as well as adjusted thinking—to adapt to manager Earl Weaver's style and approach to the game. But he soon learned that Weaver knew what he was doing and was able to draw the best out of his players through psychological mastery.

"I have a recollection of Earl taking me out of a game. If Earl could intimidate you—that was part of his strategy—if he could intimidate you, you couldn't play here. And with Jimmy Russo as the team's super scout at that time, they were very careful whom they brought into the organization. You had to be a certain type of guy. The fact that they went after me as a free agent, now, in hindsight, I guess I pretty much fit into that mold—although I didn't know it at the time. And even though I was a veteran at the time, if you didn't do it for Earl, if he didn't see it, then he didn't trust you. And so he kept taking me out of games. And I just couldn't understand why he kept taking me out, in my estimation, too early. So one day I was in the shower, just letting

Steve Stone. *Baltimore Orioles Photos*

the water run over my head. And all of a sudden I hear this click-click-click. And I look up, and there's Terry Crowley. Now Terry wasn't one of the stars of the team. Terry was basically a pinch hitter who played very occasionally. So he just came in, and he said, 'Get a towel, dry yourself off, I want to talk to you.' This was in the middle of the game. It was probably the sixth inning, at that point. I think Earl took me out after five. And Terry said, 'Look, we know where you came from. You came from the Chicago White Sox. Like most baseball teams that aren't going to win, you guys would give the game away in the seventh, eighth and ninth inning.' He said, 'You have to understand that here in Baltimore, we take the game away in the seventh, eighth and ninth inning.' He said, 'As a team, we know how to win. We don't score early, and we don't score often, but if you keep us close, we will score enough runs, and you will win more games than you ever dreamed you could win in your life.' And he was prophetic, because that's exactly what happened."

Not only did he discover that the Orioles knew how to win, and expected to win, Stone observed that his new teammates were masters of the fundamentals of baseball. They also were able to put on the mound every day a starting pitcher from a rotation that was superlative.

"As a group, they just understood what it took on a daily basis to win. They hit the cutoff man. They turned the double play when they had to. They moved the runner when they had to be moved. They did all of the little things that you hear so much about, but you never really see—in this day and age—American League teams doing. They've made the parks smaller, there's an emphasis on the home run now. The pitching probably doesn't have to be as good because teams are designed to win games, 7-5. In the game that I played when I came to Baltimore, with our pitching staff, we had Dennis Martinez. We had Mike Flanagan, who won the Cy Young Award in 1979. Jim Palmer had three Cy Young Awards already under his belt. Scottie MacGregor won 20 games the year that I won 25, and very few people heard about him because I was having the big year. We had a five-man staff that got everybody out. We kept nine pitchers on that team. Now teams keep 12, because eight of them can't get people out.

But everybody that was wearing an Orioles uniform could get people out. So Earl had many more moves off the bench than most guys did."

Stone also lauds the Baltimore front office for bringing the right players to Baltimore. And he credits Weaver with knowing how to use his players so that they performed to the maximum level of their talent.

"I just remember the front office, with Hank Peters in it and Jimmy Russo as their super scout, understanding whom to bring to the organization, and whom not to. They were a team that pretty much understood that the spare parts of a baseball team really determine whether you win or lose. It's going and getting John Lowenstein or bringing in Gary Roenicke or getting Benny Ayala. And then it's up to the manager after you get Benny Ayala to realize that he couldn't hit a fastballer, but when they put soft-tossing left-handers in the game, Benny was good for two hits. They wouldn't ask Benny Ayala, at the time, to hit a Randy Johnson-type pitcher, because he couldn't do that. But Earl put him in a situation where he could be successful. So Hank Peters went and got him, and Earl used him correctly. And they had a better knowledge of the 25 pieces of the puzzle that are a major-league roster than any group that I had ever seen before or, for the most part, afterward. So for me, it was a great experience in Baltimore. I have real fond memories of those Orioles teams."

The Orioles' success in the late 1970s and early 1980s stemmed in part from the fact that the team was composed of players who knew not only the club's system—the vaunted "Oriole Way"—but also how to work closely with one another. There was little turnover among key players, Stone noticed, and his teammates knew precisely what to expect of one another and how to work in concert.

"I remember one game that typified maybe all you want to know about the Orioles. I left the ballgame with men on second and third and nobody out. Tippy Martinez came in to relieve me. He got one out, and then he got two outs, and he pitched around Ricky Henderson and put him on first base. So he was facing Dwayne Murphy with two outs and the bases loaded. And he went, ball one, ball two, ball three against Dwayne Murphy.

And I'm figuring, 'He can't throw three strikes before he throws a ball. And then the game will be tied, and I will not win my 21st game of the year.' So he then threw strike one and strike two. And then I saw Eddie Murray take off his glove at first base. And they had the guts, the knowledge, to call a pick-off play with a 3-2 count, the game on the line, the bases loaded, in the bottom of the ninth inning. Tippy goes into his windup, throws to first base, Eddie sneaks in back of Ricky Henderson, and Ricky hasn't moved to this day. Eddie just took the ball, slapped him on the chest, and everybody ran in. The game was over, and I won my 21st game."

Weaver prepared the team for all circumstances, even the unusual. Any trick he could conjure up, any edge he could gain, the manager was willing to try. Stone marveled at the way Weaver would prepare his troops for both the routine and the unexpected.

"We had a field and a half [for spring training] in Miami. It was a very bad training facility. They called it 'little field.' We did all of these things on the little field. Earl said, 'I'm going to give you guys a play that we might not use—we use it once every three or four years. But you're going to know it. And if it comes into play, we're going to use it. Now we can only use it with runners at first and third. We can only use it when it will win the game for us. We can only use it in the bottom of the ninth or in extra innings. And we can only use it with a young, left-handed pitcher on the mound.' This situation doesn't come up very much. Now, I don't know how many teams work on that, but Earl did.

"And so, sure enough, we get in a situation with the White Sox where Rich Wortham, a young left-hander, is on the mound. And it's the bottom of the 10th, and it's in Memorial Stadium in Baltimore. They had battled us all game long. We were in a situation where we had Eddie Murray on third and Gary Roenicke on first. And they put the play on. Now they didn't have to have an extra meeting where the White Sox knew something was on. This was a sign again that you maybe use once every three years. But they knew exactly what to do. And Roenicke starts to go and then stops, and then takes off from first base. The play is designed for a young left-handed pitcher because he's going to back off the mound. And if he takes one step toward the base runner, that guy at third goes as soon as Roenicke makes his second move to second base. And the play is designed so if the pitcher takes one step at the base runner, you can't get the guy at the plate. It worked. He scored. End of game!

"Now, again, only the Orioles would work in spring training on a play that you might use once every three or four years. That's how specialized the play was. I just think they were more prepared to win than most teams, because they didn't have on paper the talent of some of these other teams. As a group, we just went out and won."

CHAPTER 28

Playing with Scissors:
Mike Boddicker
(1980-1988)

Right-hander Mike Boddicker almost became an immediate star with the Orioles upon his promotion from Rochester in 1983, helping the team get to the World Series that year—his first full season in the major leagues. In 1984 he had a 2.79 ERA and won 20 games. Entering the 2007 season, no Orioles pitcher has won 20 games since. A native of Iowa, Boddicker credits Earl Weaver with not rushing him to Baltimore and allowing him to hone his pitching skills in the minors until he was ready to make an instant impact in the major leagues.

"I was fortunate enough to have Earl keep me down in Rochester for several years [to] learn how to pitch and learn some of the stuff that young kids really don't have the opportunity to do today, because they are rushed up. So I was pretty mature by the time I got to that point. The good part about it was that [Jim] Palmer, Flanny [Mike Flanagan] and [Scott] MacGregor had been around for a while, and they made me feel like I was part of the team right away. I felt like I belonged. So it was very easy. Basically, I was still going to be sent right down after I was called

Mike Boddicker. *Brace Photo*

up in 1983. Palmer was hurt for a couple weeks. And when he came back, I was supposed to go back down. But Flanny blew out his knee, so I was there for a while after that. I was supposed to go down again, but Tippy got appendicitis. So I stayed up again. And by that time I had won about 11 to 12 games. And they said, 'Ah, we better keep you up here.' It was a great thrill. Anytime I put a baseball uniform on, it was a great thrill."

Boddicker was a star in the 1983 AL Championship series against Chicago, winning the pivotal second game on a five-hit shutout. At the time, although the game was one of the most critical in Orioles' history, he was not pleased by his performance.

"I never even thought about it. On the Orioles, everybody was basically on an even keel. Nobody got too high, nobody got too low; not too excited, not too down. Even after the first-game loss in the playoffs, Scotty had pitched a fabulous game and we lost 2-1, the clubhouse was business as usual, guys laughing, talking, no problem, 'We'll get them tomorrow.'"

Boddicker is modest about his own shutout following MacGregor's first-game loss.

"I had the fortune of pitching behind Scott MacGregor all year. I learned so much watching him, and from he and Flanny and Palmer talking to me all the time. Basically, I was just trying to do the same thing he did, trying to keep myself and the team in the game as long as I possibly could. That was my job as a starter. That's what they drove into you. So I was trying to do the same thing. It just so happened at the time that our pitching staff was locked in. *Everybody.* There wasn't anybody that wasn't throwing the ball well. So it could have been anybody in that game. I felt like I wasn't a rookie, like I was one of the guys, part of the team, doing what I was supposed to be doing. All the hype is before and after—the media and all the other stuff. Once you get between the lines, once I got out there on the hill, it's the same stuff. It's the game."

Boddicker and many other players had a special camaraderie with and love for the late Orioles trainer Ralph Salvon.

"Ralph Salvon—God rest his soul—he was a tremendous man. I loved Ralphie, he was a good friend. They told me when I first got there that the ultimate was when Ralph threw his scissors at you. I asked, 'What do you mean?' They said you have to get him aggravated enough where he gets ticked off enough, he'll reach into his pocket and throw his scissors at you. And they said Palmer's always the one to get him to throw the scissors at him. So we used to do stuff with Ralphie, like stick cups of water underneath him when he was about to sit down. And we'd put cups [of water] on the wires in old Memorial Stadium when we were in the dugout, and then we'd flip stuff up and the cups would drop down and fall on him. And Chinese seed torture, where we'd open up a pack of seeds and flip them at him, and they'd land on his big mop of white hair and just stick up there.

"Eventually, after he got full of them, he'd just shake his head and all these seeds would fall down. So one day I just kept after him and kept after him with the seed torture and said, 'I'm going to get him to throw the scissors at me.' That was my goal. I was going to get him to throw his scissors at me. All of a sudden, it was about the sixth inning, and he just snapped. I saw him reaching for the scissors, and I started running up the runway. He fired the scissors up the runway, and I could hear all my teammates yelling, 'Yeah, way to go. You got the scissors.' You had to work at it to get the scissors, and I was proud. I was part of the team.

"Ralph used to sit right up on the edge of the dugout. I remember Terry Crowley one time said, 'Watch this, I'm going to have Ralph out on the field.' He said, 'What I'm going to do, I'm going to walk up to him and fake like I'm going to punch him, he's going to lean back, and then I'm going to touch him on the chest, and he's going to roll out and look like a turtle on the field. He won't be able to get back up.' Sure enough, he walked up to Ralphie, fake punched him, Ralph leaned back, and he just touched him, and Ralph rolled right over onto the field—right during the game. We had so much fun in the dugout. I mean, we paid attention and we talked the game, but we also had fun. Baseball's supposed to be fun, and there's a lot of that missing right now."

CHAPTER 29

A True Oriole:
Cal Ripken Jr.
(1981-2001)

J ust as Brooks Robinson was Mr. Oriole for the first 20
years of major league baseball in Baltimore, Cal Ripken
Jr. personified the Orioles for most of the 21 years he
played for the team. Like Robinson, Ripken's entire
major-league career was with the Orioles. That helped burnish
his image as a true Oriole.

But Ripken really was a member of the Orioles family long
before he was signed by the team in 1978. His father, Cal Ripken
Sr., was a longtime coach and manager in the Orioles system, both
at the major-league and minor-league levels. And Junior became
a fixture in Orioles clubhouses almost from the time he traded a
rattle for his first baseball bat. If Senior was one of the primary
architects of The Oriole Way, Junior was its prized pupil. He grew
up with the idea of winning, with fundamental baseball ingrained
in his very being, and he carried that concept to great heights in
his storied, big-league career.

One of Ripken's great delights in playing for the Orioles was
that it meant he could play for his father, when Senior coached and

154

Cal Ripken Jr. *Baltimore Orloles Photos*

managed the big-league team, and also play alongside his younger brother, Bill, who was a second baseman in Baltimore.

"What was it like playing with Dad and Billy? It was really exciting when Billy was drafted and when Billy was in the minor leagues. I had already gotten used to being in the big leagues with Dad at that point. I remember the excitement as I watched Billy's stats. Then one year, in 1987, it all seemed to come together for Billy. He hit .286 at Rochester. And he got called up, I guess, to start the second half. And it was really exciting, because you started to think outside of professional baseball, a code of conduct that we were always so cognizant of. And you started to think as a family, with your brother and your Dad and hanging out. We didn't think about that too often. So when he came up, I didn't know how it would be. And certainly it settled to the same kind of thing that Dad and I enjoyed.

"When I got to the big leagues, I made the mistake of calling him 'Dad' early on. And I heard the other players kind of mock me. They'd go, 'Daa-aad.' So then I had to refer to him as 'Number 47' or 'Rip' or something like everybody else did, which was a little bit uncomfortable at that point. But it settled down, and the same was true when Billy came up. We started to act a little more professionally. Billy was just another infielder, I was an infielder, and Dad was a coach. But as the game got over, and you had a chance to go out for dinner, or you got a chance to hang out, or do those things, you went back into being a family again. And we had it for five years, or so. It's one of those things you don't fully, fully appreciate until it's not there anymore. When you look back, you realize how good it was, to have your dad around for the things you need him around for. There's two people in that clubhouse that you could trust, no matter what. And they were both related to you. Your dad was there for most everything, a catch-all, but occasionally there were a few things you'd rather confide in your brother, and kind of look for his advice or counsel. So it was a really good situation, and then all of a sudden, when it wasn't there, then you realized how special it was."

It was no longer there when the Orioles abruptly fired Senior in his second year as Orioles manager, in 1988, after the team lost its first six games. After Senior was fired, the Orioles lost 15 more consecutive games. But the bitterness Junior felt over his father's dismissal has lasted much, much longer.

"When Dad was let go after six games in '88, it's one of those things deep down inside I'll never be able to understand fully. And I don't know if anyone will ever be able to explain it to me. If six games are indicative of where you are, why was he hired to begin with? It's kind of funny, Dad was in line for a job all those years, and he was passed over a couple of times, because when Earl left, he thought that he was the next in line, but it was Joe [Altobelli]. And once he finally did get the opportunity, it seemed like we were in a situation where we were not too good talent-wise. But everybody would just say that we were just a player away, that we were so close to competing, so the expectations were high. And I guess it wasn't until the 0-21 collapse, where it came out that, 'Hey, we are going to have to rebuild.'

"Dad never was able to operate in the comfort of reality, of [people acknowledging] that we were going through some transition years, that we were looking around, that people had retired, that our talent level was considerably lower, we need to rebuild for the future. And he was never afforded that explanation. After he was fired, that was the first thing that really came out. I don't think I can ever fully understand what happened and why it happened. Here's a guy who was a lifelong Oriole, a very valued part of the minor-league system and a developer of players. He came to the big leagues carrying those same principles and the Orioles Way of teaching that still had a link to how it was done, and in the end, I guess that wasn't enough or wasn't appreciated. It was very difficult. If I had to make a decision on being an Oriole in the first month, two months or three months after he was let go, I certainly would not have been an Oriole."

Ripken learned of his father's firing in a difficult way.

"I heard it on the radio, coming into the ballpark that day. I felt disbelief, anger, shock—all of the above. It was just a horrible feeling."

The Orioles' star shortstop had felt much better about the team in 1983, his second full season in the big leagues, when

Baltimore beat Philadelphia in the World Series, four games to one. The Series ended with Ripken catching a soft line drive for the final out.

"Being from the Baltimore area, I had a great understanding of the Orioles' history and the success they had had. I was fascinated by the Orioles being able to win 100 games. That was unbelievable. How do you win 100 games? How do you get 40 games over .500? When I got to the big leagues my first year, and we started to play, we were a little bit back in the pack. But then we started to play better, and we started to make a move on Milwaukee. And you could almost see how that starts to happen. Once you start getting rolling, you run off good streaks of three wins, you win a series almost every time. You might win 15 out of 18, and all of a sudden you're in a position to believe you can win 100 games and win the division. And going down to the last game of the [1982] season we were tied with Milwaukee, that was the most exciting series I had ever played in. [The Orioles had won the first three games against the Brewers to force the tie.]

"And that kind of prepared me for the '83 season. I think it prepared all of us who went through that. Coming up that short, and then replaying the slow start we got off to, and where games could have changed at the beginning of the season—we could have been a different ball club at the end. So I think we started out the '83 season with good team resolve. And we had a good team goal to get off to a good start and make sure we won it and weren't scrambling at the end. And it seemed like everybody came together and was on the same page. If memory serves, I think we got off to a good start. We played well throughout the whole season, and I think we clinched early in September, maybe September 17.

"Then we went on to the playoffs. It was exciting for a second-year player to be playing in the playoffs and to try to capture the world championship. We ended up getting past Chicago in what was a very exciting [American League championship] series and then going on to Philadelphia. I think I tried really hard, and I was swinging extra hard and I was doing different things, as my first time in the World Series, that I think that a lot of players have done. At the same time, the other team, that you hadn't played all year, they're a little bit careful with the middle of the order, and I think I walked a few more times than I ordinarily would have if it weren't the World Series.

"While I was playing defense, with two outs in the last inning of the final game, that little hump-back liner came toward me. I thought I was going to have to jump for it, but it came down a little bit where I could catch it. That, by far, was the best feeling. There was a certain sense of gratification, satisfaction. It felt a little more complete, as a player. I guess it's more than just that moment, because it's the dreams that you had as a kid. Winning the world championship, winning the World Series, is in all your scenarios when you're playing as a kid in the backyard—that you're playing in the World Series, and you help win the World Series by catching the last out. So it made all those feelings flow together at once. It's a really special feeling, that you set out to do that, and then you actually do it."

Ripken had scores of outstanding games as an Oriole. He won two American League Most Valuable Player awards and was an All-Star 19 years, breaking the big-league record held by—who else?—Brooks Robinson. He hit for one of only two cycles in team history (Robinson accomplished the other). But his greatest offensive game had to be on June 13, 1999, in Atlanta. He had become baseball's all-time iron man four years earlier, when he had broken Lou Gehrig's consecutive-games streak of 2,130. He was almost 39 years old and many were calling for Ripken to retire. But on that day in Atlanta, Ripken set Orioles records for hits and runs, going six-for-six, with five runs, two homers, a double, six RBIs and 13 total bases.

"That was pretty wild. I remember in '83, there was a lot of times when I had five hits. It seemed like in the second half of the season I just needed to throw my bat out there. And also in the '91 season where everything seemed to go real smoothly, where it seemed I didn't have two bad at-bats in a row all year. When you get in that kind of a groove, it almost seems silly, ridiculous and easy. Hitting is actually the opposite of all those. And that night in Atlanta, I hit a home run the first time up—[John] Smoltz started that game—and then to come back and to get to the plate six times is really an achievement anyway. And to get six hits, I don't think I was ever in a position, well, I think one other time I had a chance to get six hits, in Minnesota. But everything just unfolded that night in Atlanta. I had a couple of home runs, drove in some runs. It was one of those games where we as a team couldn't do anything wrong. And me individually, I might have been able to close my eyes and swing and still get a hit. It was a good feeling."

His six-hit evening in Atlanta was especially gratifying, because Ripken's critics in Baltimore—yes, there were such creatures—said he could no longer hit or contribute meaningfully to the club at that point in his career.

"You're always facing criticism about [how] you aren't what you once were. It's kind of interesting. You gain a little bit of knowledge and experience about ways to handle a situation, but you do lose a little bit of your physical edge as you get older, naturally. It's the aging process. And sometimes you're able to play a longer time because the combination of your understanding of the game still matches your high-level skill. But, yeah, it felt particularly gratifying that that was one thing I hadn't done in my entire career—get six hits—and I was able to do it at that age, when I was still playing and competing. There was some private satisfaction that I could summon it up and get six hits at that point in my career."

The cornerstone of Ripken's career—at least in the eyes of history and baseball fans—is his surpassing of Gehrig's consecutive-games record and his own streak of 2,632 consecutive games. Ripken has been able to reflect on that accomplishment since his retirement after the 2001 season and appreciate it more fully now that he is no longer a player.

"It's alarming. It seems like it happened yesterday. Wow. Eight years ago. To me, it almost seems like it was just yesterday. So close to you, and the memory is so strong, it does seem like there's no way eight years have gone by. It's really interesting. I replay it in my mind, and I look at some of the pictures, and people give me old books and magazines that have pictures in them. They ask me to sign, and I kind of look through it and take a trip down memory lane. I seem to do that a little more now that I'm retired than when I was playing. It kind of gives you a good feeling inside, or a smile comes over you as you start remembering. But I've noticed that the real time change is in my kids. You see pictures of them when it happened, and then you see them every day—that's the only time it seems like a long time ago…

"I've said that when I'm in my rocking chair, I'll have a chance to reflect on it and do all those things. When you're playing, you really can't do all that. I don't find myself reflecting on it all the time, but I do find myself reflecting on it a little bit more—especially in situations when I go to speak and they introduce me, and that's part of my history. They play a tape, and they play a highlight of that particular night, and it kind of takes you back. So I do find myself reflecting on it a little more. It still seems magical, it still seems a little bit unreal, dreamlike, like it did not really happen. You're not sure that it happened. But when you really start to think about it and look at the pictures, I guess you know it happened. It's one of those few experiences that you do go through that is a little bit like an out-of-body experience. Like it's happening to somebody else while you're watching it."

Ripken was known for his high level of professionalism on the field. What he is less known for was his playful nature in the clubhouse. He loved to engage in high jinx, to wrestle in the locker room, to play practical jokes, to compete playfully with his teammates in games other than baseball.

"That's some of the things that you do miss the most about playing. You do have the moments between the white lines, and that's been on TV, and you kind of live through the successes and the failures of those moments, and you know how it feels. But when you look back, you miss traveling, being with the guys on the road, hanging out with them, and the little pranks and the joking that goes back and forth. A lot of times, it's just how you choose to spend your time, how you choose to deal with the pressures that go along with baseball. I think for a lot of us, we consider ourselves having never had to grow up—because you're in baseball. So some of the behavior sometimes goes right along with it.

"When I think of Ben McDonald, I think of him as one giant big kid. And some of the games we played. You'd make tape balls in the clubhouse, and some of the pranks you'd play with the clubhouse kids. Ben McDonald was a regular player in our tape ball games after hours that we had in Minnesota. A lot of times, especially when we went through those hard rebuilding years, whereas most of us derive a lot of pleasure and satisfaction out of playing the game when you play it on an everyday basis, when you lose—when you lose at the level we were losing at—you weren't getting the fun. So, as a way to kind of deal with that, we decided to play a game afterward when nobody was in the stands—just for ourselves, so we could actually have fun. So that's where tape ball came from. We'd make our tape balls in the training room and then do all the things you wished you could do on the field. Maybe smile smugly at a home run or run around the bases and scream at the pitcher or do some things that you refrained from doing. And it was really a great thing.

"The clubhouse kids, in Minnesota especially, they would put headbands on and they would come down dressed, and we would make lineup cards from the extra lineup cards. And we'd kind of theme it. And we'd take some drinks down to the field, like it was a picnic out in the park. And we'd just start playing. We'd play right in the dome. They had a couple of low lights on that you could see with, but occasionally we were able to get a little bit more light on so you could see better. We'd use a fungo bat and the tape balls. We didn't need baseballs. And we basically played without gloves. We had bases down there. We put home plate out toward center field, so we could actually use the fences. You could shape the balls any way you wanted. I would cheat. I would press them together like a pancake, sometimes, when they weren't looking, like I was rubbing the ball up. That was nicknamed 'saucer ball,' because you could throw it like a flying saucer. And it gave a little less area in which you could hit it. I pitched sometimes. We all changed positions. We'd have four on each team. We rotated around covering the bases. It was really a version of a pick-up game.

"Remembering baseball a certain way as a kid, and kind of simplifying it, that was our way of having fun. And it was amazing going down there and playing. And I guess it was amazing that nobody got hurt. I felt better, going home at 2 o'clock or 3 o'clock in the morning from the Dome. And we'd actually play two games. So I guess if you're adding up 'The Streak,' you could throw in a few more tape ball games. So the number can grow, if you want."

CHAPTER 30

Tee Bone:
John Shelby
(1981-1987)

John Shelby came to Baltimore as a fleet center fielder with a good-field, no-hit reputation, and that's exactly how his Orioles career proceeded. He was with the Orioles for seven seasons in the 1980s and participated in some big games for the team. But he never ripened into the star that some Orioles had hoped he would become.

Shelby had one of the more interesting nicknames in Orioles history—Tee Bone.

"I was on the rookie ball team in Bluefield, and I'd always been addressed growing up as 'Tee.' My middle name is 'Tee.' So I told the players to call me 'Tee.' And some clown, a left-handed pitcher from Alabama, started calling me 'Tee Bone.' I hated it. But every time I went by him, he'd say, 'Tee Bone.' Then every other guy starting doing it, and all I would do was ignore it. So when the season was over, I thought that was the end of it. But when I got to spring training the next year, more people started calling me 'Tee Bone.' So instead of ignoring them, I started acknowledging them. And that's how I got stuck with it. The guy who gave me the name, I don't even remember his name now; he never made

John Shelby. *Baltimore Orioles Photos*

it. That was the last I saw of him that year. Now I love the name. And sometimes I accidentally even sign stuff, 'Tee Bone.'"

Shelby's ascendancy up the Orioles' farm system coincided with the minor league career of Cal Ripken Jr.

"My second year in Bluefield, I had a chance to talk with Ripken when he was young and raw. I still remember one time, he was playing shortstop, and it seemed like balls just constantly went through his legs. He was a rookie, and I went up to him one time, and I told him, 'I'm getting tired of catching all your balls that go into center.' He kind of looked at me, and he thought that was kind of harsh for someone to jump on a rookie. But look what happened to him after that. So I think I set him on the right course."

When Shelby came to Baltimore at the end of the 1982 season, he had no idea that the Orioles were fighting for their lives to remain in the pennant race and catch first-place Milwaukee. Although the Orioles didn't quite make it that year, the final series of that season was one of the most exciting in Baltimore baseball history. The Orioles hosted the Brewers for a four-game series, beginning with a doubleheader on October 1. Milwaukee led Baltimore by three games at the time, meaning the Orioles would have to win all four to win the pennant. The Birds swept the doubleheader, 8-3 and 7-1, then blasted the Brewers in Saturday's game, 11-3. Tension was immense for the final game on Sunday. Not only was it to be the day on which the pennant was decided, but Earl Weaver had previously announced that it would be his final game as Orioles manager. There were 51,639 fans crammed into Memorial Stadium. The Orioles lost the game 10-2, but the fans stayed long after the final out to give the gutsy team and its even more gutsy manager a boisterous send-off.

Had it not been for a play Shelby made a week earlier in Milwaukee, however, the Orioles likely would not have been able to challenge the Brewers for the pennant on that final weekend.

"Al Bumbry was the center fielder when I came up to Baltimore. The only thing I was worried about was making it to Baltimore and being the center fielder. I acknowledged that Bumbry was there, but my whole focus and goal was to be a leadoff hitter for the Orioles playing center field. Fortunately I got called up briefly in '81, and I got a chance to experience a little bit of the big leagues. Then, at the end of '82 I went up for about 29 to 30 days, somewhere around that. And although I've been in two World Series, I never experienced anything like the end of the '82 season. I guess the high point for me was when I first came up. We were in Milwaukee. I didn't really pay attention to the standings. I threw a guy, Bob Skube, out at home plate in the eighth inning. It was a one-hopper, right to Dempsey. At the time they called me up, I had bone chips in my shoulder and couldn't really throw. I was going to have surgery after the season. And Earl Weaver, when they called me up, he asked me if I could throw. And I told him that if I didn't have to take infield practice before the game, I could make a throw. I think I played in some 20 games, and that was the only throw I had to make. It's still so vivid and clear in my mind, as though it had happened today. And as I was coming across the field, I noticed the whole stadium was silent. And as I came toward the dugout, Eddie [Murray] and everyone else was standing on the top step. And I'm running in like, 'What's going on, I just threw a guy out at the plate, no big deal?' And these guys were picking me up. We won the game. And after the game, I've got a million reporters around me talking about a throw. So Cal's locker is next to mine, and after all the fuss kind of died down, he looked over at me and said, 'You don't know what you did, do you?' I said, 'No, I really don't.' He said, 'That throw you made helped win the game, and now we go back to Baltimore and have two final series with the Yankees and the Milwaukee Brewers [with a chance to win the pennant].'

"Back in Baltimore I wound up getting my first big-league start, my first big-league hit in the Yankees series. And then I got my first big-league home run and a curtain call in a game against the Milwaukee Brewers in the final series. I've been in some ballparks where there's been excitement—and I don't think there was anything more electrifying than being in Yankee Stadium—but at the end of the 1982 season, that was when Earl Weaver was retiring and we had the final back-to-back series against the Yankees and the Milwaukee Brewers. I don't think there was a seat left, even on top of the roof. That place was so packed, and every play the fans were so into it. And we won all those games until the last one of the season. And there was the thrill of watching the fans stand and acknowledge Earl at the end of the season. Everybody wanted to win it for Earl. We just had a fantastic team, with good teammates. I've never experienced anything like it. We won the World Series the next year, my rookie year, which was a dream come true, but that '82 series at the end of the year, I never have experienced anything like it."

Shelby played with the team that went to the World Series in 1983.

"We had a good ball club. Basically, we just went out and won. The guys were mature, they knew how to play, and the atmosphere was comfortable. Even in games when we were down one or two runs, Eddie would say stuff like, 'Hey, let's go, let's snatch it.' The momentum just took over. I don't know how many games we lost, but it seems like we won them all."

The 1983 team was not only very good, but it also was very funny. If Rick Dempsey was the crown prince of that 1983 team, and Mike Flanagan its stand-up comedian, John Lowenstein was its court jester.

"People used to send us cakes all the time. I don't know where they used to come from, but people sent them to us in the locker room. And if there was a cake in the locker room, with no name on it, they would always call John Lowenstein over to check the cake out to see if it was any good. So he would walk over with a bat on his shoulder and all of a sudden just rear back and slam the bat down through the middle of the cake. The cake would fly all through the locker room, and everybody would be screaming. And he'd look at it, and he'd say, 'That was a good one.' That was hilarious, watching him do that stuff.

"Mike Flanagan was another who was a constant comedian. We were playing in Cleveland once, and it was freezing. Some of the guys had those ski masks on, and all you could see were their eyes. And I remember Todd Cruz putting one on his head and bragging about himself. And when he walked away, Flanagan said, 'It don't matter. They still know how to pitch to you.' He just had funny stuff, a lot of short one-liners, [that would] just keep you in tears."

"One of the best times I had was when we won the World Series in Philadelphia. The reporters didn't know what we were up to, but [Cal] Ripken and I had this thing where we'd fill our cups up with champagne, and we'd walk around and see one of the reporters trying to stay dry. And we'd walk up, and we took turns. Whoever had the champagne in their hand would walk up to the other guy, and we'd be like, 'No, no, no!' And just as you'd get ready to throw it, the guy ducks and, oh man, we soaked so many people. That was a blast. That was just awesome. We soaked so many people who were trying to stay dry. Ripken and I still talk about that."

Ripken and Shelby, now first base coach for the Pirates, also spent time together in the minor leagues. Shelby sometimes was the victim of Ripken's practical jokes.

"We had a team party in Miami Beach, before we were in the big leagues, when we were in 'A' ball. I had these Converse tennis shoes. I'd always clean my shoes and keep them in excellent condition. And I'm out trying to body surf, knowing nothing about it. And Ripken grabs my shoe, and he's pretending he's going to throw it in the water. I'm out there getting mad, saying, 'Man, don't do it.' And he throws one in. It starts sinking, and I get it, and I'm coming out of the water, and I am hot. And he's screaming and telling me that my other shoe's in the water. And I'm like, 'No, I'm not going for that.' And I get up on the beach, and my shoe was gone. And you talk about hot. I think from then on, from 1979 until I got to the big leagues, he always furnished me with shoes. He gave me a good supply. I don't know if I ever forgave him, but I took all the shoes that he gave me. I'd always come in and find new shoes in my locker. We wore the same size at the time, but it was tough to forget those Converses. They were my high school shoes—they were valuable. I kept them clean. They were awesome. He was just playing around. He knew that I didn't know what I was doing out there in the water. And when I went under to get one shoe, he threw the other one in. So I had to walk barefoot. And I hated walking barefoot in the sand."

CHAPTER 31

Traded for Himself:
Tito Landrum
(1983; 1988)

O utfielder Tito Landrum played with the Orioles only briefly—less than two months—and went to the plate fewer than seven dozen times in a Baltimore uniform. Yet he left an indelible impression on both Orioles fans and in the club's history book with one single swing of the bat. That swing produced a pivotal home run in the 10th inning of the fourth and deciding game of the 1983 American League Championship Series against the White Sox in Chicago, sending the Orioles on to the World Series. The Orioles had acquired Landrum in a late-season trade with St. Louis for a mysterious "player-to-be-named." He hit .310 for the Orioles, but by the next season he was back with St. Louis.

"I was the player-to-be-named-later in my own trade. I didn't find that out until [Joe] Altobelli told me when they had the All-Star game in Baltimore [in 1993]. That was kind of amusing—to be traded for myself. The whole experience in Baltimore was wonderful for me. I came over and met the team in Toronto. I walked in and [reliever] Tim Stoddard, a big, naturally strong guy, palmed my head and almost lifted me up off the floor. He said,

Tito Landrum. *Brace Photo*

'Welcome to the team, little man.' Eddie Murray then came over and said, 'Do you have a place to stay?' I said, 'No.' He offered his house, so I stayed with Eddie. And, of course, Eddie's best friend at the time was Cal Ripken, so I was a kid in a candy store.

"Leading up to the home run in the ALCS, I think Eddie hit a ball to right center that didn't make the fence. He crushed it, but the wind was blowing so hard that day, it didn't make it. Carlton Fisk did the same thing. So the biggest surprise to everybody in that park, including me, was the home run that I hit. I don't even remember really touching the bases, but I remember touching home, being congratulated, and then Eddie Murray slapping my hand. It was all a dream come true for me.

"I can count the home runs I hit in my career on one hand, but I can remember the one against the White Sox very well. I hadn't been making good contact, so I sat beside our hitting instructor, Ralph Rowe, right before that at-bat. I said, 'Ralph, can you give me some pointers here?' He said, 'You know what. You are the type of hitter that tries to hit the ball up the middle and in the alleys. But you're trying to pull the ball today. Why don't you go up there and try to hit one between the gaps.' So thinking about that, I went up there, and the ball was in a good place, and I happened to connect real good."

The Orioles went on to win the Series and then, almost as quickly as he had appeared with the Orioles, Landrum was gone again, dealt back to St. Louis.

"It was disappointing in the sense that you get to know guys, and you feel comfortable around them the very first day. I don't like to use clichés, but it really was a family atmosphere. These guys had seemed to grow up in the minor leagues together. They got along well. Nobody really enjoyed being in the limelight singularly; they wanted everybody to get the credit they deserved. So it was just a wonderful clubhouse experience and a wonderful on-field experience for me. And it was difficult in the sense that we had just won a World Series, and now I was going back to St. Louis."

CHAPTER 32

Soft-Tossing Lefty:
Jeff Ballard
(1987-1991)

J eff Ballard was a graduate of Stanford who played for
the Orioles in one of their most forgettable seasons and
one of their most memorable ones. He joined the
notorious 1988 team after it had lost its first 21 games
of the season. And he pitched for the 1989 squad that surprised
the baseball world by reversing its 1988 performance and went
down to the final weekend of the season with a chance to win
the pennant. Ballard led the team that year with 18 wins. He was
brought up to the Orioles in 1988 shortly after Cal Ripken Sr.
was fired as manager and Frank Robinson was named to replace
him in the dugout. Ballard, who now runs a highly successful oil
company in Montana, found Robinson's style as manager very
perplexing.

"Frank was a man of few words as a manager. I can't remember
who the third pinch hitter at the time was, but for a time the other
two were Joe Orsulak and Pete Stanicek. When Frank wanted a
pinch hitter, he'd look at the three of them at the end of the bench.
The three of them were at the far end of the dugout. Frank would
be at the home plate side of the dugout. So when he wanted a

pinch hitter, he'd stare down there and kind of go, 'Hey,' and point down toward them. He wouldn't yell out a name. He'd motion his finger toward the guy he wanted to pinch hit. But the three of them were all sitting together and they couldn't tell which one of them he was pointing at. They'd look at him again, and he'd point down their way with a little more authority. And they'd all say, 'Me?' because they didn't know which one of them he meant. He'd finally do it a third time with still a little more authority. And he'd do the same thing every time he wanted a pinch hitter. He'd never say a name. It was really kind of amusing—watching three guys stand up at the same time and wonder which one of them was going to hit. As a pitcher, I'd just sit there and watch the whole transaction. The three of them finally decided they'd just take turns."

Ballard was a left-handed pitcher who lacked a blazing fastball. That didn't help speed him up the organizational ladder in an era when club officials felt the fastball was the most important weapon in a pitcher's arsenal.

"During my years with the Orioles, they went through several transformations. After the '87 season, the word from the front office, at least the word we were getting as players, was that the front office was disenchanted with the fact that we pitchers didn't throw very hard. So they decided to go out and get free agents or make trades for guys who could throw hard. They ended up bringing hard throwers to spring training like Jose Mesa, Oswald Peraza, and Jose Bautista. And those guys got all the innings in spring training. I had pitched fairly well the previous September, so I thought I'd get a chance in spring training. But I hardly was given the opportunity to pitch. Eric Bell had 10 wins in '87. He threw kind of like me, with a good breaking ball and change-up, throwing mostly in the 80s. But he hardly got a look in spring training, even though he had 10 wins the previous year on a team that wasn't very good.

"So in their mind, the team was going to go with the hard throwers. It got down to the final days of spring training, and they needed to cut one more pitcher. And none of those guys who threw hard had pitched very well. But with just two days to

Jeff Ballard. *Baltimore Orioles Photos*

go, they had Jose Mesa start a game, and they'd already made the decision that Mark Williamson was going to be cut. They already told him that he was going down, but they kept him around until after the game, just in case they might need to use him that day. Mesa went out and threw 12 straight balls to start the game. So they changed their minds and decided to keep Williamson, even after they'd told him he was going down. It made you wonder how the front office went about making decisions. Then, of course, they ended up losing 21 straight games to start the season, and they made all kinds of changes. So it's kind of interesting to watch the front office, what kind of philosophy they have and how they go about making decisions."

Ballard had pitched for the Orioles at the end of 1987, but he didn't make the Opening Day roster in 1988, at least in part because he couldn't throw hard enough to please management. He was called up in May, after the 21-straight loss debacle, but he never felt confident of his spot on the roster until he happened to read a blurb in the newspaper one day.

"I might be critical of Frank as a manager, the way he didn't communicate much. But there's one thing I'll always be thankful to him for. In 1988 I got called up on May 19, after the big losing streak. I pitched pretty well when I came up. I went 4-4 until July. And then I went into the tank. I was terrible. I lost my next five games. And the press was starting to get pretty brutal. They asked Frank when the team was going to send me down. They said I couldn't make it up in the big leagues. I had no communication with Frank or the coaches. Every day I kept coming to the park thinking this was going to be the day they were going to send me down. But each day no one talked to me, so I thought each new day, 'I guess I'm still here.' Then one day a reporter asked Frank what they were going to do with me, when they were going to send me down to Triple-A. Frank told him, 'Jeff has nothing else to prove at the Triple-A level. He's not going to go anywhere now. He's going to stay here and pitch, and he'll have to prove it here that he can do what he can do right here.' Frank didn't say a word to me. I read it in the paper the next day. But it gave me the confidence I needed. I finally could relax and just go out and pitch and not worry that every day was going to be my last.

"So then I pitched two complete games and one shutout. All of a sudden I knew I wasn't going to go anywhere. I was able to relax, and I got my confidence back, and I finished the season strong. The next year in spring training Frank told me that I had made the team and that I should just get ready for the season. So it was a big thing that I read what he had to say about me in the paper. I wish he had told me to my face, but at least I read it and was able to relax and stick around."

The Orioles entered the final three-game weekend series of the year in 1989 trailing first-place Toronto by a single game. Ballard was asked to pitch the series opener in Toronto.

"The biggest game I was ever involved in was the first game of the final series of the season in Toronto in 1989. We were one game behind the Blue Jays, and it was a Friday night, and it was my turn to start. I was pitching against Todd Stottlemyre up in the Sky Dome. Phil Bradley hit the very first pitch of the game from Stottlemyre for a home run. The dugout was euphoric. With one swing of the bat, we changed the atmosphere at the park from the fans all yelling to our dugout up and yelling. But that was the only run we scored. I went out on the mound in the bottom of the first after we scored that one run. I'm sure there are many games where you're probably nervous, but you don't realize that you're nervous. But in that particular game there was so much on the game. I took my warm-up pitches, and 60,000 Sky Dome fans decided they wanted to be heard.

"Lloyd Moseby was the first hitter, and Al Clark was the home plate umpire. Jamie Quirk was catching for us. He called for a fastball on the first pitch. It was so loud in the Sky Dome that the place was vibrating. It really was like electricity was running through the place. Your hair was standing up on end. I remember starting my windup, and I couldn't feel anything. I thought, 'Oh my god, I'm going to throw the ball, and I can't feel anything, I don't know where it's going to go. Maybe I'll throw it into the press box.' And then the ball left my hand, even though I couldn't feel it, and it went over the corner of the plate, and Al Clark put his hand up for strike one.

"That was the one time in my career I really knew I was nervous. When you're out there on the mound, you don't have the luxury to burn off your nerves. You can't run around to get relaxed. And that game had a playoff atmosphere. You've played 159 games, and it all boils down to this. I left the game in the ninth inning, and I was winning 1-0. No one scored after the first pitch. I had a runner on first base and one out. They pinch-ran Tom Lawless at first base. And we brought in Gregg Olsen. He struck out the first guy, Lawless stole second, and he stole third. Kelly Gruber was up. And Olsen had a 1-2 count on Kelly Gruber. Gregg had the best curve ball in the league that year. But he threw one then that was a little too nasty. It broke and hit the plate and jumped over Jamie Quirk's head, and Lawless scored the tying run. Then they scored the winning run in the 10th.

"You wonder what might have happened had we won that first game. It was exciting. That's probably, even though we lost, one of my favorite memories from Major League Baseball. You play hard in the dog days of summer, but it's a job. It's a routine. But all of a sudden, you get down to the end of the season fighting with the Blue Jays for the pennant, and every day you get to the park, it's incredibly exciting. That's the way baseball should be. Opening Days are like that, too. You open up the season, and everybody has high hopes. But pretty soon it gets into a routine. But that September it came down to the final weekend. It was great. And I'll always have those memories.

"The thing about that team was that being so young and coming out of nowhere really made that real special. Young guys like Brady [Anderson] and [Steve] Finely and Mike Devereaux. We had real speed in the outfield. And we didn't have one big-name pitcher. Gregg Olsen was awesome that year. And that was my big year. And it was kind of neat to see. We pulled together as a team, all around Cal. He was the one real star. It was neat. We really were close-knit. We had a lot of fun together, both on and off the field."

CHAPTER 33

All in the Family:
Bill Ripken
(1987-1992; 1996)

Bill Ripken was much more than Cal Junior's brother and Cal Senior's son. He was the starting second baseman for the Orioles for a number of years, teaming up with his brother, who was playing short at the time. Bill was an excellent fielder—no one could go back on a pop fly better than he could—and he was as sound a fundamental player as his big brother. He didn't have much pop in his bat, but he did hit .291 in 1990. He was something of a jokester and, though serious on the field, liked to approach life in a light-hearted way. When he first came to the majors, he acknowledges that it was comforting to join a team that already included his brother as its star shortstop and his father as the manager.

"I think the one thing I kind of got a heads-up on before I was called up was when I was in Rochester, and [Cal] Junior called me one night. He said I might want to get some of my things together and be ready to move. You never want to get too excited about that sort of thing, because it might not happen. Right after Junior called, Pete Stanicek got called up to Rochester, and he also played second base.

179

"That day I got to the ballpark—John Hart was the manager—and I saw that Stanicek's name was in the lineup. I said to John, 'Am I not going to play anymore?' And he just gave me this grin. He called me into his office after the game and said, 'You're going to the big leagues.' I had all my stuff ready, so I got in the car and drove the next morning straight to Cal's house. I went to the ballpark early, because I was probably as giddy as a school boy. I'd been in the park many times before and been to the clubhouse before. But it's a very different feeling when you walk into the clubhouse and you're looking for your own locker. I knew where Cal's locker was, and I knew where Dad's was. I saw No. 3 there where my locker was going to be, and I was pretty happy about that because I was No. 56 in spring training.

"That day was probably the earliest I ever got dressed for a game. [Cal] Senior stuck his head out of the manager's office and said to come in there. He shook my hand and said, 'Congratulations, you're playing tonight.' That was a good thing, because I didn't have to sit and wait anxiously. Looking around the locker room and seeing your brother and father made things a little easier. You had someone you could always lean on.

"I leaned on Junior more than Pops. Either if he was the manager or the coach, there were times when you could sit down and talk with him, but there was much more time to talk with a teammate than a coach or manager. So I talked more with Junior. But on technical things, you could talk with Dad.

"When I was in the minors in Charlotte, N.C., I could call Dad. You'd usually call when things weren't going right. So usually you talked with him when things were on the down side. I'd tell him I went 0-for-4 and didn't hit pitches I should have, so what was I doing wrong. He'd say, usually, 'You're pulling out your front shoulder.' Or he'd say, 'In batting practice tomorrow, go up there to home plate and concentrate on keeping your front shoulder in and hit the ball hard. It doesn't matter where.' That was a technical thing. While you're in the big leagues, and he's throwing batting practice, you could rely on him to keep the mechanics of your swing sound. I'd rely on him for that, and I'd rely on Junior for the everyday stuff of playing big-league baseball."

Bill Ripken. *Brace Photo*

If Ripken was proud to join the same team that already included his father and brother, he believed his teammates liked the idea as well, even if they sometimes would joke about the three Ripkens being together.

"When you get to that point, I don't think you're teased. But they'd make certain jokes. When I got called up, [Mike] Boddicker and [Mike] Flanagan and Eddie [Murray] and Fred Lynn were there, veterans with a good sense of humor. They would take shots at us, but I think they thought it was pretty cool. It was the first and only time in major league baseball that a manager managed his two sons. And I think those guys admired Senior as a manager and what he had done for baseball. And Junior was already established. So I think that it was pretty cool that another family member could come up to the big leagues and play for Senior. There's no way anyone gets called up to the big leagues as a favor."

Like most players, Bill Ripken remembers his first big-league home run—as well as the greeting he received after he crossed home plate—as if it happened yesterday.

"You never forget the first home run. It was in Kansas City, a day game, and it was hot—like 137 degrees on the carpet. I'm going up to home plate to hit off Buddy Black. Two guys are on, Alan Wiggins and Kenny Gerhart. With one ball and two strikes, I'm hitting second in front of Cal, and he throws a fast ball down and in. I knew I hit it good. In Rochester, at the time I was called up, I didn't have any home runs. I hit the ball good, and then I heard Junior in the on-deck circle, yelling, 'Arrrgh.' He's hit a lot of these. And that ball was gone.

"I remember running around the bases. Before I went to hit, I stood in an ice bucket in the dugout because it was so hot, and as I was running around the bases, water was squirting out of my shoes. I shook hands with Kenny and Alan, and then Cal and Eddie. The first guy in the dugout was Senior. And the rest of the guys gave me the silent treatment. I gave them some choice words, something that was caught on television. My mom still doesn't understand exactly what I said, because she doesn't want to understand. But it was pretty cool that after I touched home plate and ran toward the dugout, the first guy there was Cal, and then you have Eddie and then you have my dad. Those were three pretty good ones."

When the Orioles went on their horrid, 21-game losing streak to open 1988, Cal Senior was fired as manager, a week into the season. It would be more than three weeks before the team finally notched its first victory of the year, during a night game in Chicago. Bill Ripken remembers that game well, and not just because of the big, maiden win of the year. The game came after a night on the town, and it ended for Ripken with a dangerous thud to the head.

"We were coming out of Minnesota and had just lost our 21st game in a row. The flight was a businessman's special. We got into Chicago and pretty much had a lot of fun that night as far as boys being boys, having fun out on the town. It was Cal and me and Kenny Gerhart. The next day we had to go to Comiskey and play the White Sox. And we're facing Jack McDowell.

"I was feeling pretty good at the plate, and I think Cal hit two out. I came to the plate and set myself to sacrifice bunt, and I got hit by a pitch square in the coconut. I eventually got carried off the field because I was knocked out. Cal was the first to come up to me at the plate. When I finally came to, Cal said I was lobster-eyed. Carlton Fisk was the Sox catcher, and he put his glove under my head. Cal said my left eye went off to right field, and my right eye went to the backstop toward the upper deck.

"After I got carried off, back in the clubhouse, the doctor asked me how I felt. I said, 'It hurts, but I don't know if it's from the ball hitting me or the 50 Coronas I had the night before.' William Schaefer was Maryland's governor then, and when we won that first game in Chicago to break the streak, Schaefer sent us crabs in the clubhouse. I don't know how they got there so fast. But I couldn't participate and eat any of the crabs, because I had a concussion, and my head was killing me, and you can't have crabs without beer, and I couldn't have beer. So I had to watch everybody else eat crabs and drink beer and celebrate our first victory of the year. I was sitting there thinking, 'This is just great.'"

CHAPTER 34

Wrasslin' Gators and Ripkens: Ben McDonald
(1989-1995)

B en McDonald was a big, young right-handed pitcher out of Louisiana State University when the Orioles chose him as the very first overall selection in the 1989 amateur draft. He soon after became the first pitcher in team history to win his first five starts in the big leagues. McDonald showed flashes of brilliance in the rotation, but arm problems derailed his progress, and after the 1995 season, he was headed off to Milwaukee, his Orioles career abruptly at an end.

Modern-day big-league clubhouses are far more button-down serious than they were in years past. But McDonald was a throwback, gangly in both body and attitude, a product of the bayous who brought southern charm and boyish playfulness to the Baltimore locker room. He was noted for his wrestling proclivities, taking on alligators in the Louisiana swamps as well as Cal Ripken Jr. in the Orioles' clubhouse. McDonald and Ripken had side-by-side lockers, and their corner niche in the Camden Yards clubhouse was where most of the good fun took place in the early 1990s. Both were big and strong, and they liked to mix it up with one another.

Ben McDonald. *Baltimore Orioles Photos*

McDonald was an avid hunter and fisherman, and one day, during a heavy rainstorm, he brought some of his love of the outdoors to Camden Yards.

"They had some drainage problems when Camden Yards first opened, especially in the dugout. When it would rain a whole lot, the water would just pour down out of the stands and off the field and fill up the dugout. It would even go back up into the tunnel and toward the batting cages near the clubhouse. The drains just didn't work very well back then. One day we had a really hard rain, and there was a delay of the game. It was one of those rain delays where not much was going on. Outside, the water just started filling up the whole dugout. It got to be about four feet deep in there. Some guys still had their fishing poles in the clubhouse that they'd left there from spring training. Down in Florida, we had the poles to go fishing. Well, I thought it might be kind of fun to get one of the poles and bring it into the dugout. So I just slipped in during the delay and got one of the poles. There also were some Oriole fishing hats in the clubhouse that they'd given away to the fans a few nights before. So I put one of them on as well. I went back out then into the dugout and sat there with the pole and dropped the line into the water. As deep as the water was, I wouldn't have been surprised if I had caught something. It was pretty funny.

"Me and Cal had some really fun times. Wrestling with Cal was one thing we did. We also loved to play tape ball. We actually had this one game where we'd slug each other in the arm—not our throwing arm, but the offside arm. I was amazed at Cal, because for some reason, he never got bruised. Then we had this other game where we'd see who bruised the most. So one day we'd slug each other in the arm real hard, about five or six times each. Then we would see who'd have the biggest bruise the next day. I came to the ballpark the following day with a bruise the size of a softball. But Cal, he barely had a bruise on his arm at all. I just couldn't believe it. He and I would wrestle all the time, too. But I knew I had to be a little careful because of 'The Streak.' It wouldn't look too good if I hurt him, if I cracked a finger or bruised his hand, and then he wouldn't be able to play in a game.

"One game I was pitching in '93. I was pitching really, really well in this stretch, but I wasn't getting much run support. In this one game, it was in the seventh inning, and I had this really big blister on the middle finger of my pitching hand. They tried to bandage it up. Most people didn't realize it, but I pitched with a blister in 28 out of 34 starts that year. I often had to wear a bandage on the finger, which was technically illegal, but there was nothing I could do. So in this game, our trainer, Richie Bancells, was looking at the finger. It was bleeding, and he was putting on the tape and bandage, trying desperately to stop the bleeding. He saw Cal standing nearby, and he called him over. Richie said, 'Junior, Ben's bleeding to death. Go up there and hit a home run so we can get Ben out of the ball game.' Cal went out there onto the field and up to the plate and hit the next pitch out of the park. I said, 'Boy, he sure made it look easy.' I got the side out that inning, and then [manager] Johnnie [Oates] took me out of the ball game."

If there ever was such a thing as the Three Musketeers in the Orioles locker room, it was McDonald, Ripken and Butch Burnett, a Camden Yards clubhouse attendant who is legendary among major league players for his lovably good-natured ways. It was not unusual for McDonald and Ripken to pull some kind of a prank on the almost always unsuspecting Burnett.

"We'd do all sorts of stuff with Butch. Butch always surprised me, how strong he was. One day he was picking on Junior and he was picking on me. People always had the impression that we would be the ones to always pick on Butch, but sometimes it was the other way around. Anyhow, this one day he was picking on us, so we picked him up, and told him if he didn't quit it we'd put him in the whirlpool. Butch couldn't swim, so he was scared to death about being put in there. But he kept going at it, so me and Junior and [Rick] Sutcliffe picked him up and put him down on the trainer's table and taped him up, from the feet all the way up. Then we carried him over to the whirlpool. It didn't have any water in it, but we put him inside it and began to fill it up with water with a hose, like we were going to fill it to the top. Butch was scared to death, but he was so strong, he broke through all the tape and was able to get out. Another time we put him on the trainer's table and tied him up. We put QDA—an adhesive—on his head. Butch shaves his head, so there's no hair there. Then we let it dry up a bit, and we poured powder on the top of his bald head. The poor guy had to run around with a white head for three days after that. We had some good times with Butch. I fly him down to Louisiana every Thanksgiving, and he spends about five or six days with me. We go over to my land in Mississippi and we go hunting and fishing and riding four-wheelers. We have a great time together."

CHAPTER 35

Eight Steps to the Plate: Jack Voigt
(1992-1995)

I n the early 1990s, Jack Voigt was an outfielder who wanted to do everything exactly right while he was with the Orioles. He wanted to look like a major leaguer, act like a major leaguer, and play like a major leaguer. But he had a sense of humor about himself, and he took a lot of ribbing from his teammates.

"The years I was there, who was there? [Mike] Devereaux, [Brady] Anderson, Ben McDonald, [Mike] Mussina, [Jeff] Tackett, [Chris] Hoiles, all those guys like that, and of course, Cal [Ripken]. When I first got there, I think one of the biggest things that they liked to drop on me as a rookie was, I was real big on drinking Coca-Cola. I always had this big plastic cup, and I'd go up in the clubhouse and get my ice and put the Coke in it and come back down on the bench. It was one of those big, 32-ounce, like Big Gulp cups. I'd be walking back down in front of the bench, and they'd all take their turns throwing handfuls of sunflower seeds at my cup. And by the time I'd get to the end of the bench, my cup had all the sunflower seeds floating on the top. So, now, of course, the Coke is bad, so I had to throw the

Coke out and walk back up to the clubhouse and do it again. It got to the point where I'd walk by with my hand over the Coke. Everyone knew when I started to walk up and in, usually between innings, that was everyone's time to get their guns loaded with handfuls of sunflower seeds. Eventually that migrated to pieces of gum and everything else being thrown in there.

"I learned a lot, not just about the game of baseball, but how to do the things that you were best at doing, and not trying to do things you weren't capable of. And I learned a lot about that from talking with Cal. Cal was the type of guy you could ask him questions, and you could talk about things. You had to pick your spots, when to do it. But there were times when he volunteered information to me. I think he saw that I worked hard and respected what I did for the ball club while I was there. We took a cab ride or two to the ballpark.

"One time specifically I remember in Minnesota, he called me at the hotel and said, 'Do you want to go over to the park?' because he and I always went early. I wasn't going to turn down a ride to the park in a cab with Cal. So we went, and he told me there was a left-hander throwing that night, and I always played against lefties. And he said, 'You know, you're playing tonight?' And I said, 'Yup.' Johnny [Oates] had already told me a couple of days ahead of time that I'd be playing. And he said, 'You know, they're throwing a right-hander tomorrow.' And I said, 'Yeah.' And he said, 'You're not going to be playing tomorrow.' And I said, 'Well, yeah, I understand that.' And he says, 'You get what I'm saying here? You're going to play today. And unless something strange happens, you know you're not playing tomorrow. So don't let tomorrow creep in on today. Just do what you have to do today, there's no pressure, and do the things that you do, get your hits where you can, move your runners along where you can, hit your cut-off men like you do, and do the things that Jack Voigt does to help Baltimore win.' And I went out that night and got three hits; one of them was a double that started a rally.

"It was nice being around that type of guy who was willing to share information. Harold Baines was another one like that. Bainesie, you could talk to him about hitting and stuff. Everyone thought Harold was real quiet, and in a way, he was, but he didn't

Jack Voigt. *Brace Photo*

say anything unless he needed to. He was one of those quiet leaders by example. It was nice to be around guys like that and learn the so-called "Oriole Way." The Oriole Way, it's not like they reinvented the wheel. It's just that The Oriole Way was a way of being professional. You went about your job, you wore your uniform correctly, you acted correctly, and you were respectful of not only your teammates and the staff, but also of the umpires and everyone else.

"To play the game of baseball is really just getting yourself into a comfort level, and it's learning your routines. Harold Baines had a routine before games. We'd do our flips downstairs in the cages. Some days Harold would get in there and take 10 balls, 10 little flips, and hit 10 line drives right off the center of the "L" screen and say, 'I'm good.' And he'd walk out, and he was ready for the game. Other days it would take 20 minutes, and he'd hit 10 line drives, and we'd say, 'Okay, Harold, you're done. Our turn.' And he'd say, 'Nope, I just don't feel right.' And he'd do what he had to do to get ready."

Voigt was a man of many, many superstitions, and almost as many nicknames.

"It really wasn't superstitions as much as my way of preparing myself and my brain, in my mental approach, that I'm doing the same thing again, and the next time I'm going to do the same thing again, and the same thing again. And eventually, in a way you can almost trick your brain to tell yourself that this isn't any different situation than I haven't been in before. That's what makes your good pressure players or your good clutch players so good. They learn to control the emotion, they don't let the emotion control them.

"Some of the things I did—I'd take the same number of swings in the on-deck circle with the doughnut, and then I'd take the doughnut off and take the same number of swings without it. I'd try and take the same number of steps between the on-deck circle and home plate before I stepped in the circle. I'd go through the same type of mannerisms in the box. I'd tug at my left shoulder and then touch my hat. And then tap the bat one time and around. And a couple practice swings and things. My number of steps I tried to make to the plate was eight. It might have been superstition. Every player has some type of mannerisms. Look at Nomar Garciaparra. He has the toe taps and everything else, pulling on his gloves. He probably doesn't even realize he does it any more. That's just his thing, his way of getting a rhythm.

"I guess you could say I was superstitious, but more than anything else, it was getting into a habit and then going with it. I also tried to never step on the lines, but that was because I really didn't want to leave footmarks everywhere on the field. If you stepped on the line in the minor leagues, it was lime, not the painted stuff. A lot of times when my wife and kids were up in the summertime, if I had a big night, we'd always try to have the same lunch the next day—her beef stew or some type of Latin dish. I guess that's superstitious, but why mess with it?

"One of the first nicknames I got was 'Cotton,' because I was always talking. I was always asking questions, always talking, always wanting to talk baseball. So some guys started putting cotton in their ears because they were getting earaches from hearing me talk so much. I had another nickname, 'Super.' Rafael Palmeiro gave me that name, and also, 'Perfect,' because I always tried to do everything right. Even taking infield, I always wanted my throws to be perfect, one-hop throws and everything else. Jamie Moyer gave me the nickname 'Roy Hobbs,' because when I faced him in the minor leagues, he had trouble getting me out. I don't know why. I was probably one of the easiest guys to get out."

One of Voigt's biggest thrills as a major leaguer, as for many ball players, was his first home run. But Voigt also was taught a couple lessons of humility after hitting his first home run for the Orioles.

"It was June 4, 1993, in Camden Yards, and I was starting against Randy Johnson. It was the infamous weekend of the fight that happened the next game, Saturday night, between Mike Mussina and Bill Hasselman. It was Friday night, and my wife—my fiancée at the time—was there for her first time ever in the states seeing a major league game. The first time up, I think I hit the ball off my wrist bands, Randy got in my kitchen so bad. I hit a little dribbler up the first-base line, and Tino Martinez came over to field it. I guess he thought I was going to run nice and easy into a tag, and all of a sudden I slid around the base and got the bag with my hand—safe. I got a base hit. Then, the second time up, I homered to left off Randy.

"Later in the game, there was a rainstorm where we got a delay, where the dugouts always filled, and then we came back. It was still raining, and I hit a base hit to right field to score Devereaux with the winning run in the bottom of the 10th. Even though they didn't keep game-winning RBIs anymore, it was my first major-league game-winning RBI and my first major-league home run, all in the same night. So after the game, there were about 50 reporters all around my locker, and I was thinking, 'Boy, this is cool. This is the big leagues here.' And cameras all around. And everybody's yelling, 'Cotton, Cotton,' behind me, all the players.

"And a couple minutes after the press all left, one of the clubhouse kids came over and said, 'Jack, there's a guy out at the door of the clubhouse that's got your home run ball. They saw on the board that it was your first major-league homer, and he wants to give it to you.' And I said, 'Oh, all right.' I had been wondering if someone would notice that. So I go out and meet the guy and say thanks for this and that. And I say, 'Can I get you anything, one of my autographed bats or a signed ball or something, I'd like to give you something for you taking the time to bring me the ball.' And he says, 'Yeah, I'll tell you what I need.' So he tells me. So I walk back into the clubhouse, and Cal's walking by, and he says, 'How was your press conference?' I said it went okay, and this and that, and I said, 'The guy who caught my home run ball, he just brought it over, and he's waiting outside in the tunnel.' And Cal said, 'Oh, that's nice. Are you going to give him an autographed bat or something?' I said, 'Yeah, I told him I'd give him an autographed bat. But he said he wanted one more thing, and he'll give me the ball.' And Cal said, 'Yeah, what's that?' And I said, 'He wants an autographed bat from you.' So I ended up giving him one of my autographed bats, and something autographed by Cal, to get my home run ball—my first major-league home run. So that was humbling real quick.

"Then, the next day, we come in that Saturday. That was when Rick Sutcliffe and Fernando Valenzuela were on the team. My locker was right there as you came in on the corner, with Johnny's office right there. When I had come in I checked the board, the way I always checked to see if I was in the lineup. It was quicker for me to tell if I was in the lineup by checking from the bottom of the card up, rather than look from the top down. So I could glance at it real quick. So I came in, I knew I wasn't going to be in there because a right-hander, [Chris] Bosio, was throwing.

"So I'm not in the lineup, and I'm sitting there getting dressed at my locker, and I kind of see Sutcliffe come in and stop and look at the lineup. He stops at my locker and says, 'How can you not be in there today?' I said, 'They have a right-hander throwing.' He said, 'You got three hits, the game-winning RBI, your first major-league home run off "The Unit." How can you not be in the lineup? I'm going to tell Johnny you want to be in the lineup.' He turns his head and says, 'Johnny, Jack can't believe he's not in the fucking lineup tonight.' And I look in and say, 'Johnny, I didn't say anything about it.' And Sutcliffe said, 'You just told me right here you can't believe you're not in the lineup after what you did last night.' Just burying me. Rolling me right out of the bus."

CHAPTER 36

The Moose:
Mike Mussina
(1991-2000)

During the 10 years he was an Oriole, Mike Mussina was the team's best pitcher, as well as one of the top starters in the American League. He led the Baltimore staff in wins in six of those 10 seasons and in ERA eight times. Even though he played for some poor Oriole teams during the '90s, his winning percentage of .645 is the club's best ever for a pitcher with 70 or more decisions as an Oriole.

He was spectacular in the Orioles' last postseason appearance in 1997. In the American League Division Series he twice beat Seattle's Randy Johnson, and in the AL Championship Series against Cleveland he was even more magnificent, although he was unable to pick up a win because the Orioles' offense was nonexistent in the two games he pitched. In four postseason starts in 1997, Mussina pitched 29 innings, allowing only four earned runs (1.24 ERA) and 11 hits while striking out 41.

In a sense, that was indicative of most of his years with the Orioles. Despite his superlative pitching, he often received little run support. He also was denied a 20-victory season, winning 19 twice and 18 twice, once missing out only because a reliever blew

Mike Mussina. *AP/WWP*

a lead in a game at the end of the season that would have meant victory number 20 for Mussina.

His first game in the big leagues, on August 4, 1991, was something of an omen of things to come.

"They called me up the last game in July. The team was coming into Chicago from Seattle. I got to watch a couple of games before I was asked to pitch. So at least I could sit in the stadium and watch the team and get a little familiar with things. I lost 1-0 to Charlie Hough. He threw a five-hit shutout against us. I gave up four hits, and three of them were to Frank Thomas.

"For losing a game, it was a good way to start. I was thinking about all those things that go through your mind in that situation. You wonder if you can cope with it, if you can compete, if you can do what they expect you to do. It was a new experience. I knew it was the pitcher's mound, I knew it was the ball field, but it was different because it was the major leagues. And, sure I was nervous. I probably was nervous more than just the first time, probably for two or three games after that.

"The next game was my first home start. And my third or fourth start I had to pitch against Nolan Ryan. And there was a lot going on at the time. Cal [Ripken] was having a good year, but the team was struggling. It was the Orioles' last year at Memorial Stadium. But it was a great experience for me. Of course, there was the adjustment period of getting used to playing and standing with people you were used to watching on television. It was an adjustment, but it was great going out there and playing with Cal, as well as the guys I've played with since, like Eddie Murray and Mike Flanagan. You get to put on the same uniform as these guys and travel on the same plane and be teammates."

Mussina believes his 1997 playoff performances against Seattle and Cleveland were among the best games he pitched in Baltimore.

"I think that whole playoff stretch in '97 was some of the best I pitched up to that point in my career. It was four starts in a row. The first two games were against Randy Johnson. And then the last two games against Cleveland in the ACLS, I think I gave up one run and seven hits [it was actually just four]. But we just couldn't get any runs. I held them to one or no runs, and we couldn't get more."

Yet the playoffs were far from the only time that Mussina—one of the smartest pitchers ever to play for Baltimore—had glistened on the mound as an Oriole. He pitched three one-hitters for Baltimore. One of those gems, on May 30, 1997, was particularly heartbreaking. He took a perfect game into the ninth inning against Cleveland, only to have it spoiled by a one-out, slicing single to left by Indians catcher Sandy Alomar. Mussina then struck out the next two batters to win the game, 3-0.

"I didn't even know what was going on for a while. But then you get that late in the game and the crowd is really going wild. In about the sixth inning, I knew I hadn't pitched out of the stretch. Games like that are like a blur because you don't have to think about a lot. You're never in a jam, you never need to make a big pitch to get out of an inning or stop a threat. It just sort of happens. I knew what was happening, what was going on, in the eighth and ninth innings. But at the time, it was only a 2-0 game. So at the same time you get excited, you know that in a matter of two pitches, not only might the historical moment get away from you, but the game as well.

"I threw the pitch I wanted to throw to Sandy Alomar, but he just got enough of the bat on it to get it to left field. Of course, you have second thoughts about that pitch forever. But I certainly don't go to the mound ever expecting not to give up any hits. It just so happened in that game the only hit I gave up came in the ninth inning. It wasn't that much of a deflation for me after the hit. I was still two outs away. After the hit, you fight that feeling of deflation off for the three or five seconds it lasts, and then you have to go and get the next guy out."

CHAPTER 37

20 Years at Camden Yards: The Good, the Bad, the Ugly

On a brilliantly sunny April 6, 1992, Oriole Park at Camden Yards made its debut and launched a new era of major league baseball in Baltimore. The much-beloved but dowdy Memorial Stadium, home to the Orioles for 38 years, was abandoned for a downtown ballpark that shone—and still glitters—like a gem. It is arguably the finest pure baseball stadium in the country today.

Camden Yards has set the standard for every major league park that has been built since. Its retro look and feel, brick facade and steel trusses, pure sight lines and unobstructed seats, purposeful avoidance of symmetrical dimensions, and its downtown location have changed the way planners and architects have approached the construction and location of new parks. For the three previous decades new baseball stadiums were usually constructed in suburbia or near interstates, they were round or oval bowls that often also accommodated football, and they had little real distinguishing characteristics. Camden Yards changed all that. It is not just a stadium. It is a baseball park.

It also had the good fortune of being located not only on the precise spot where Babe Ruth's father once owned a tavern, but also adjacent to the century-old, 1,016-foot brick B&O Warehouse—the longest building on the East Coast. The warehouse, which runs lengthwise behind the ballpark's right field wall, has come to serve as a spiritual, aesthetic and physical ballast to the park. When Camden Yards first opened, people wondered who would be the first batsman to hit the brick structure with a home run ball. They're still wondering. At a distance of 439 feet from home plate, the warehouse remains unscathed by a fly ball hit during a major league game. It has thus taken on the character of a mythical figure, becoming as much a part of Camden Yards lore as Cal Ripken.

Through 2011, 57 home run balls cleared the right field wall and landed on Eutaw Street, just short of the warehouse facade. Of those, 23 were hit by Orioles and 34 by opposing players. (The longest home run ever hit at Camden Yards arced 465 feet to dead center and was propelled off the bat of Darryl Strawberry.)

Attendance soared during the first decade of Camden Yards' existence. The club routinely drew over 3.5 million home fans a year. In 1995 the Orioles' home attendance even exceeded that of the New York Yankees and Mets, combined. The park was usually filled to the brim, especially during 1996 and 1997, when Oriole teams were American League powerhouses and went on to the postseason playoffs. For four consecutive summers, Baltimore led the American League in home attendance.

But even as Camden Yards has retained its beauty and its dignity (it has never been denigrated by having its commercial naming rights sold or by being plastered with excessive advertising signage) its attendance has plummeted alongside the Orioles' place in the AL East standings over the past decade and a half. In the mid-1990s the Orioles drew an average of more than 45,000 people a game to Camden Yards. In 2010 and 2011, fewer than 22,000 fans came to an average game.

Fans who became accustomed to perennial Oriole playoff runs grew disenchanted by steady last place finishes by the hometown boys, leading up to the 20th anniversary season of Camden Yards in 2012.

A team that once had been baseball's winningest club for almost two decades did not recorded a winning season from 1998 through 2011—14 years of losing baseball.

In each of 13 consecutive years, from 1968 through 1980, the Orioles had at least one 20-game winner. From 2000 through 2011, they never had a pitcher win as many as 16 games.

Perhaps the most definitive sign of the Orioles' dramatic decline over the past decade and a half can be discovered by looking at the club's representation on the American League All-Star team. From 1966 through 1999, the Orioles placed an average of three players on the All-Star squad, and in four of those years, had at least half a dozen All-Stars. But in all but one of the 11 years from 2001 through 2011, the Orioles had only one All-Star representative. From 1966 through 1999, the Orioles could boast of 42 starters in the All-Star games. In the past 11 years they have had but two starters. And two of the Orioles' All-Star representatives over the past few years were journeyman ballplayers—George Sherrill and Ty Wigginton— who made only brief stops in Baltimore, yet still managed to put more All-Star worthy numbers on the board than anyone else on the team.

There have, of course, been great moments at Camden Yards, the kind of thrilling and historic baseball happenings and memories that kids (and adults) will carry with them for the rest of their lives. The first was the Orioles' 2-0 win over the Indians in the first game ever on Camden Yards soil, when Rick Sutcliffe threw a five-hit shutout against Cleveland.

Probably the most glorious memory of Camden Yards etched in the minds and hearts of Baltimore baseball fans during the park's first two decades was set on September 6, 1995, when Cal Ripken surpassed Lou Gehrig's long-held record for consecutive games played. President Bill Clinton and Vice President Al Gore were in attendance when Ripken broke the standard for athletic stamina and longevity by playing in his 2,131st consecutive game. And just as he had done the previous night, when he tied Gehrig's mark, Ripken—with an uncanny flair for the dramatic—hit a home run to put a lovely exclamation point on his achievement.

A year to the day after Ripken's historic feat, Oriole great Eddie Murray (during a brief return to the team near the end of his playing days) blasted the 500th home run of his career at Camden Yards. Seven years later Murray was named to baseball's Hall of Fame, where Ripken joined him four years thereafter. When Ripken played his last game on October 6, 2001, after 21 years as an Oriole and exceeding Gehrig's streak by more than 500 games (before sitting out a game in 1998), 48,807 fans came to Camden Yards to pay tribute to the beloved hometown star.

There were two years of exciting playoff games at Camden Yards in 1996 and 1997, when the Orioles virtually had an All-Star at every position. Players like Ripken, Roberto Alomar, Rafael Palmeiro, Brady Anderson, Bobby Bonilla, and B. J. Surhoff stood alongside pitchers Mike Mussina, Jimmy Key, David Wells, Scott Erickson, and Randy Myers.

Mussina, easily the greatest Baltimore pitcher in Camden Yards history, was stellar in those playoff games. And with his notably seamless pitching motion, in which he would swoop down like a crane before going into the set position, the savvy Mussina still holds the record for most wins at Camden Yards.

Oriole pitchers hurled four no-hitters before the club relocated to Camden Yards, but none since they have inhabited the park. The only no-hitter in Camden Yards history was thrown by the Red Sox' Hideo Nomo on April 4, 2001. Mussina came within a ninth inning line drive of a no-hitter at Camden Yards on May 30, 1997. The Oriole right-hander had retired the first 25 men he faced before yielding a single to the Indians' Sandy Alomar. He then struck out the final two batters of the game.

There were other notable performances by Oriole players over the last 20 years, as well.

Melvin Mora set the club record for best batting average by hitting .340 in 2004. During the same season, shortstop Miguel Tejada knocked in 150 runs to establish a new seasonal RBI mark for Baltimore. In 1996, the unlikely Brady Anderson, a leadoff man who never before or after hit as many as 25 homers, broke the Orioles' home run record, with 50. And the amazing Cal Ripken, near the end of his career in 1999, set a club mark for most hits in a game—six—though he did not collect those hits at Camden Yards, but in Atlanta.

Two Orioles have hit for the cycle at Camden Yards— Aubrey Huff in 2007 and Felix Pie in 2009—both against the Angels, who also were Baltimore's opponents during Ripken's momentous game in which he eclipsed Gehrig's record.

During his first stint in Baltimore, Palmeiro put together what were probably the most productive five consecutive offensive seasons in Orioles' history—averaging 36 home runs and 111 RBIs (in a span that included two strike-shortened seasons) and hitting .292. Palmeiro still holds the record for most home runs at Camden yards—124.

There also has been the weird and the bizarre, like the time when rain-soaked fans got to witness the classic scene of pitcher Ben McDonald, a product of Louisiana bayou country, playfully casting his fishing rod one evening in the Orioles dugout, which had been flooded in the midst of a game during a mid-summer storm. At one home opener, a sudden snow flurry enveloped Camden Yards, and a pop fly down the right field line temporarily disappeared from view amid the descending flakes.

In 2008, the Orioles probably wished that blue laws were still in effect. From April through July, they lost games on 15 consecutive Sundays.

Sadly, most of the records set by the club over the last decade or so were on the negative side of the ledger.

Part of the problem was instability at the top. The Orioles made a string of poor choices when it came to naming field managers. Pilots like Phil Regan, Ray Miller, Lee Mazzilli, Sam Perlozzo, and Dave Trembley simply were overmatched and not up to the job. And before players had much of a chance to adjust to each one's style, they were gone. General managers, scouting directors and player development directors also came and went with such frequency that the Orioles never were able to a develop a consistent, coherent philosophy that could take them back to the days of the Oriole Way and Oriole Magic.

As the Orioles floundered, a chicken-and-egg question plagued the team. Until the recent appearances of Brian Roberts, Nick Markakis, and Matt Wieters, it seemed as though the

Orioles were unable to draft and develop a single position player (with the possible exception of the oft-injured and eventually traded Jeffrey Hammonds) who made a meaningful contribution to the major league club since the signing of Cal Ripken and his brother, Billy Ripken, three decades earlier.

Why was the front office so inept at producing big league players? Was it poor scouting that led to abysmally inadequate draft choices, or was it woefully misdirected player development philosophies and practices that turned otherwise potential stars into career minor leagues. Whatever, the Orioles squandered year-after-year of high draft choices. Usually, they concentrated on signing pitchers and annually would hype these strong young arms as the next coming of Jim Palmer. But after Mussina, all the supposed golden arms turned out to be tin: Adam Loewen, Hayden Penn, Mike Paradis, Beau Hale, Richard Stahl, Alvie Shepherd, Wade Townsend, Matt Hobgood, Chris Smith, Matt Riley. They all were flops.

Because general managers, scouting directors and farm directors departed with alarming alacrity, some blamed the plague on owner Peter Angelos, the only constant over the past two decades and the man ultimately responsible for the team that is put on the field each year. Angelos might not have been involved in the drafting and nurturing of players, but he was the one who pulled the strings and was responsible for the hiring of those who ran the team. The Baltimore lawyer headed a group that bought the Orioles from previous owner, Eli Jacobs, in August of 1993.

One of the saddest moments in recent Oriole history, and something of a metaphor for the team's descending fortunes, was the death of Mike Flanagan by his own hand on August 24, 2011. Flanagan had been a superlative Oriole pitcher—a one-time AL Cy Young winner— during the team's glory days and a much beloved icon for both teammates and fans. He also was an Oriole through and through, a man who moved to and resided in Baltimore from his native New England, an avid collector of Oriole memorabilia, and the last Oriole to pitch in Memorial Stadium (a distinction he cherished). Besides ranking in the top five in Oriole pitching history in wins, strikeouts, complete games, and starts, "Flanny" served the team as pitching coach, co-general manager, vice president, and broadcaster. While his death took fans and former teammates by shock, and while suicide is not generally the product of a single event or happenstance, some who knew Flanagan said he was deeply saddened at how poorly the club had performed in recent years and how he had failed as a front office executive to turn things around for the Orioles.

Another true-blue Oriole whose death touched Baltimore baseball fans deeply was that of Elrod Hendricks in 2005. Hendricks was a popular catcher for the Orioles during at least parts of 11 seasons in the 1960s and 1970s and was a coach for the team for 28 years. No one in history wore an Oriole uniform as long as Hendricks, and no one did more as a goodwill ambassador to promote the team in the Baltimore community. Hendricks and Flanagan were part of that old breed of Baltimore Orioles who were said to bleed orange.

Yet written into the DNA of baseball and its fans is the character trait of hope. And even as the Orioles have failed to be competitive in the tough American League East over the past 14 seasons, the seeds of optimism still are implanted in the soil at Camden Yards. Quality players like Wieters, Markakis, and center fielder Adam Jones give the Orioles a foundation to build upon. In the minor leagues, a top prospect, 19-year-old Manny Machado, is being primed to take over one day as Baltimore's shortstop and continue the team's tradition of superlative players at that position. And while the minor league pitching continues to be questionable, there is hope—yes, that word again—that young right-hander Dylan Bundy can begin restoring the Orioles to their former status as a team noted for its outstanding arms.

Through all that has occurred over the past two decades—the optimism, the pessimism, the wins, the losses, the great players who have trod upon the grass at Camden Yards and then departed, the memories, both sweet and sour, that have lingered—the ballpark remains a source of great pride to Baltimoreans. The one thing that it has lacked, in its brief history, is to be home to a World Series. That is a chapter that Baltimore fans are still hoping—and hoping—to one day read.

EPILOGUE

The stories shared by the players in this book weave together an anecdotal history of five decades of Orioles baseball. But they certainly don't attempt to constitute a complete chronicle of the Orioles and the more than 8,300 regular and postseason games they have played over the past five decades.

So many exhilarating, quirky and intriguing moments and games emerged during those 53 seasons that no single book could catalogue them all. Yet while many great stories might go unmentioned in these pages, they remain enshrined forever in the collective memory of Orioles fans.

For instance, there was the game on May 18, 1957, for which the Orioles and White Sox agreed beforehand that regardless of the score, the contest would end precisely at 10:20 p.m. so the Sox could catch an overnight train to Boston. Chicago held a 4-3 lead going into the ninth inning, and seconds were ticking down to the moment when the White Sox would be declared victors. All Chicago pitcher Paul LaPalme had to do was shuffle about on the mound for a few extra seconds, hold onto the ball or throw a wild pitch to Orioles leadoff batter Dick Williams, and the win was in the bag. Instead, LaPalme threw one right over the plate, and with virtually no time left, Williams whacked the ball—and the game's final pitch—out of the park. The contest thus ended at 4-4. The Orioles wound up winning the rematch.

Then there was the infamous, incredible eighth inning of April 17, 1993, when three Orioles base runners—Brady Anderson, Jeff Tackett and Chito Martinez—all ended up on third base at the same time. Martinez was immediately sent down to the minors, never to appear again in an Orioles uniform.

One damp and thunderous summer evening almost 40 years earlier, young Willie Tasby shocked his teammates and fans by playing center field without his shoes. He worried that the metal cleats might attract lightning and electrocute him.

A huge swarm of gnats almost kept Hoyt Wilhelm from winning his ninth consecutive game in Chicago on June 2, 1959. The insects chased the knuckleballer off the mound in the first inning and refused to disperse even when the White Sox grounds crew attacked with spray guns. It took the setting off of fireworks on the mound to scare the pests away so that Wilhelm could get down to work and conquer the hometown Sox, 3-2.

One of the most electrifying victories in team history came on June 23, 1964, at Memorial Stadium, where the fledgling Orioles mounted a remarkable eighth-inning comeback against the Yankees. Trailing 7-2 with two outs in the bottom of the inning, Baltimore scored seven times and wound up gaining not only an incredible and unexpected 9-8 win, but also the confidence that they finally were on an equal footing with the boys from the Bronx. It was one of the first games in which the Os merited a standing ovation from their faithful followers.

It was not until two years later, however, that the Orioles were able to show not only their own fans but the entire world that they were the best team in baseball. They won the World Series in 1966 thanks to Frank Robinson, who came over in a winter trade from Cincinnati and won the triple crown that year. Robinson quickly showed the Orioles how good he was on May 8, when he became the only player ever to hit a home run completely out of Memorial Stadium. Six weeks later, he demonstrated that he could also play pretty nifty defense when he jumped high above the right-field barrier in Yankee Stadium to steal a potentially game-winning homer in the bottom of the ninth inning from New York's Roy White, toppling into the seats but still grasping the ball.

Four decades later the Orioles were robbed of a chance to get to the World Series at almost the identical spot in Yankee Stadium's right field during the American League Championship Series game. A young fan, Jeffrey Maier, leaned over the railing and caught a ball headed for the glove of Orioles outfielder Tony

Tarasco. Umpire Rich Garcia improperly declared the ball hit by Derek Jeter a home run, enabling the Yankees to tie the game and then go on to win it in extra innings.

Each Baltimore fan—those who went to but one game or those who attended hundreds—has a chest full of memories from the green fields of Memorial Stadium and Camden Yards.

Thrills and chills didn't take place only on the baseball field, however. Paul Richards, the man who forged the Orioles into a winning club when he served the organization as both manager and general manager in the 1950s and early '60s, provided plenty of pyrotechnics from the front office and the dugout. He once came close to pulling off a trade of his entire ball club for the 25-man roster of the Kansas City Athletics. He also had a promising young outfielder fake an injury by intentionally running into the stadium wall in the hopes that the injury would dissuade other clubs from drafting the player. Richards, nicknamed the "Waxahachie Wizard" after his baseball smarts and his hometown of Waxahachie, Texas, is the man who implanted the seeds into the young franchise that would later sprout into the team that for years was the most successful in all of baseball.

Though Richards was indeed a wizard, he was not the only great mind to lead the Orioles, nor was Frank Robinson the only great athlete to wear an Orioles uniform. The baton has been passed from GM to GM, from manager to manager, from player to player. The Orioles are one long continuum, generations of ballplayers melded into one another. The tradition transmogrifies from one team to the next, year after year, season after season. And the tales of the men who wear the Orioles uniform are never-ending. Their exploits this year and the next and the season after that will be remembered and then dispatched to future generations of Baltimore fans. Players come and go, and their successes and failures and eccentricities are lodged into memory. But the team goes on playing. New legends are born each year.